95 FOX

THIS WAS MY CALL LETTERS IN PATROL AT WEST HOLLYWOOD SHERIFF STATION

Love-ET' KayPulls

95 Fox
Copyright © 2019 by Love-ET' KayPulls

All rights reserved. No part of this publication may be reproduced, distributed, or transmitted in any form or by any means, including photocopying, recording, or other electronic or mechanical methods, without the prior written permission of the author, except in the case of brief quotations embodied in critical reviews and certain other non-commercial uses permitted by copyright law.

Tellwell Talent
www.tellwell.ca

ISBN
978-1-77370-836-2 (Paperback)

TABLE OF CONTENTS

ACKNOWLEDGEMENTS V

MORE ACKNOWLEDGEMENTS VI

DEDICATION VII

95 FOX IX

CHAPTER ONE 1

CHAPTER TWO 3

CHAPTER THREE 9

CHAPTER FOUR 18

CHAPTER FIVE 22

CHAPTER SIX 27

CHAPTER SEVEN 41

CHAPTER EIGHT 43

CHAPTER NINE 68

CHAPTER TEN 74

CHAPTER ELEVEN 81

CHAPTER TWELVE 86

CHAPTER THIRTEEN 95

EPILOGUE 97

CATCH OF THE NIGHT
By Paul Harman (West Hollywood Deputy 1968-1972) 101

STUDIO ONE
BY Chief Roy Brown, Retired 103

MY TIME
By Commander Lynda Castro 105

WEST HOLLYWOOD STORIES 1973-1976
by Marla Lohneiss (Blomer) Dike 107

CADET ON PATROL
By Bob McCarty 113

THE COLORS
By Assist. Sheriff, Duane Preimsberger, retired 115

THE CRIME FIGHTERS
By, Assist Sheriff, Duane Preimsberger, retired 136

A LOOK AT THE PAST REMEMBER?
By Duane Preimsberger, Asst. Sheriff, retired 152

THE LITTLE MOTHER
By Duane and Judy Preimsberger 168

MORNING WATCH FOLLY'S
by Duane Preimsberger, Assist Sheriff, retired 200

THE CRIPPLED GUY
BY Duane Preimsberger, Assist Sheriff, retired 203

WALDO THE TALKING DUCK
by Duane T. Preimsberger, Assist. Sheriff, retired 211

SCUBA KING
by Duane T. Preimsberger, Assist. Sheriff, retired 216

WEST HOLLYWOOD STATION 1971-1972
Sgt. John Jackson, LASD, retired 220

415B CHASEN'S RESTAURANT
by Gary Fitzgerald 223

ELVIS & I
by Steve Lee 225

SMELLS LIKE A DEAD GUY
By Duane Preimsberger, Assist. Sheriff, retired 228

ABOUT THE AUTHOR 233

ACKNOWLEDGEMENTS

To the other 11 female deputies that were first in patrol:

> West Hollywood Station
> Carole Freeman
> East L.A. Station
> Maryfran Baker
> Norma Zinn
> Altadena Station
> Judy Allen Preimsberger
> Charlene Rottler
> Lakewood Station
> Barbara Birkland
> Jeannie Miles
> Elaine Minnis
> Judy McGrath
> Kathy Wade
> Carol Perry

MORE ACKNOWLEDGEMENTS

It wouldn't be right for me to not acknowledge:

Gary Huffman, my training officer and dear friend still today.

Captain Dennison, with a great sense of humor.

Chief Roy Brown, for thinking enough of me to take me with him to see Darden's wife and for always treating me so fairly

Mike Grimes for making everyone laugh at me when I slept on the floor, under his cot.

DEDICATION

I am dedicating this book to my dearest friend and encouragement and faith in me, I would never have become a deputy sheriff, or one of the First Women in Patrol. Geo's name is pronounced George, but he never liked it spelled that way. I guess he was an "individual" too.

95 FOX

These were my call letters while working in patrol at West Hollywood Sheriff Station, and boy do I have some stories. I was one of the first twelve women in the United States to ever be assigned to work in a police patrol car. Up until that moment, women were delegated to inside desk jobs.

Regardless of the gender, jobs like these are all about communication. Military, airlines, and police spelled out a letter to make it clear what letter they were saying. Although the objective was the same, they were different for each entity. As an example, the Sheriff's Department used these alphabetical names:

A = Adam
B = Boy
C = Charlie
D = David
E = Edward
F = Frank
G = George
H = Henry
ETC.

In most cases the corresponding names to the letters were men's names. In my case, I was assigned to work a 95 car which stood for the West Hollywood Station. F or Frank denoted what part of town I was to patrol. With me being one of the first women in the field, the sergeant thought it would be funny to refer to me as Fox instead of Frank. So, from my first day in patrol, I was always referred to as 95 Fox.

My uniform, or lack of one, also became an issue. While the men were given proper uniforms, the women were not. The Sheriff, Peter J. Pitchess, was concerned that we would look too masculine in a pants uniform with a gun belt and police safety equipment. So, the women were sent out to patrol in miniskirts and a white blouse. Believe it or not, we were not even issued a Sheriff's identification patch to wear on the shoulders of our blouse.

Oh, but it gets better. The Sheriff also thought the women should wear high heeled shoes, panty hose and no gun belt or any safety equipment. We were each given a shoulder purse to carry a 38-caliber revolver inside. You can just imagine how impossible it was to get your gun under those circumstances. Imagine, trying to chase a suspect over a block wall without kicking off your high heel shoes and hiking up your mini skirt over your ass in order to throw your leg over the wall. Since I knew that all of the general public and my fellow deputies were going to see my underwear, I spent a fortune on matching ones. I wore one pair under my pantyhose and an identical pair over my pantyhose. I didn't want anyone to make inappropriate remarks about the looks of them. Men can be very catty.

Did you see her granny underwear? Her panties had holes in them. Oh NO! I couldn't have that.

I have deliberately left out the names of most of the people I mention in this memoir. I also omit exact locations and times, to protect the innocent. Other than that, I write the unfiltered facts about my experiences. You can take it or leave it, but…you better believe it.

CHAPTER ONE

When I was about seven-years-old, I was walking home from elementary school and came upon a man parked at the curb, frantically masturbating. Although, I had never seen this before, I was aware that whatever he was doing, it was intended to shock or embarrass me. That really pissed me off, so I decided to embarrass him! I just stood there, pointing my finger at him and began laughing uncontrollably as loudly as I could. His eyes opened wide, and he jumped into the driver's seat and sped away. I was pretty savvy, even as a little kid.

It happened again when I was about nine-years-old, coming home from school. I got about one house away from mine, and a man parked in front of the house next door, beckoned me over to his parked car, asking me to show him on his map where a certain street was. I could see that he was doing the same thing the other man had been doing, and he wasn't wearing any pants. I thought, What an idiot! Most adult women can't even read a map! Why would he expect a little kid to be able to read it! I was two-years-older, and two-years-smarter and figured, No way asshole! I took off for my house, yelling over my shoulder, "My mom knows how to read maps, I'll go get her for you." By the time I reached my driveway, he was already driving away. Of course, my mom was at work, and I knew that, but I figured I would be safe from him in the house. My mom had never told me not to talk to strangers, so I never told her about it because I was afraid, I would get in trouble for it.

I recall a time when I was about six-years-old, I was roller skating around the block, slipped, fell, and broke my left arm. It was a compound fracture and the bone was sticking out of the side of my arm. I didn't cry out in pain, I had never seen one of my own bones sticking out before. I did cry, when the Dr. removed my cast, because when I looked at my arm, it was all shriveled up and skinnier than the other arm, and it had long hair growing on it. The rest of my body was completely hairless. It really freaked me out!

CHAPTER TWO

By the time I was thirteen years old, I already knew that I would become a policewoman. I even went so far as to go on a local "Bandstand" TV program and announce it to the world. Not long after that, a Burbank, California motor cop, his pregnant wife, Thelma and their kids moved in across the street from me. His name was Geo Fairchild. He didn't like to spell out George, even though that was how he pronounced it. If there was any doubt – and there wasn't - I knew from the moment I met Geo that I would also become a cop. I owe my entire career to Geo.

Babysitting was something I did for them every chance I could just to be closer to a real cop. He was only charged thirty-five cents an hour or usually for free. I loved Geo, his wife Thelma, and their three kids. Mostly, I loved his boatload of police books. He had books on police procedures, detective investigations, and lots of books on forensic science. I tore into those books with a voracious appetite and couldn't get enough of them. Sometimes I would just go over to their house to read his books. His books on forensics and patrol were of special interest to me. For those reasons, I was very careful not to use drugs or get into any trouble.

Aside from Geo, I also babysat for other neighborhood kids. One lady had eight kids. Did you hear me? EIGHT kids! Once, when all of the husbands – yes, I said husbands – decided to go off on a hunting trip, my mother convinced the other neighborhood ladies to leave all TWELVE of their kids with me to babysit. This was for thirty-five cents an hour while they ran off to Las Vegas. One of the children was a three-month-old baby.

Can you imagine the faith these women had in me at the age of thirteen? Well, I didn't let them down. Even though all of the kids - with the exception of the newborn – came down with the flu and threw up everywhere, and two kids got a bloody nose, (No, I didn't punch them.) I had the innate ability to know what needed to be done without being taught. Somewhere in my vast thirteen-year-old knowledge, I knew enough to wash the blood out of their sheets, pillowcases, and pajamas with cold water.

When the women returned home in three days, they paid me my three dollars and went on their merry way. I didn't care about the money. If they only knew, I would have done it for free. I loved all of those kids.

Can you imagine parents leaving their kids with a thirteen-year-old now? They would have been lynched if it was found out. But that was a different time. I was raised in the early 1950s and the world was so much different than it is now. It was a time when we all were responsible for everyone and everyone's kids. A mother could punish someone else's kids and no one batted an eye. Moms would stand on their porch when it started to get dark and yell for their kids to come home. And that's all it took to make them come running.

I helped teach most of the neighborhood kids, that I babysat, the basics of growing up. I taught them things like, how to roller skate - with "old time" roller skates – mind you, ride a bike, and to play jacks. Does anyone even remember what jacks were today? Let me just say this about jacks, you never wanted to step on one with your bare feet.

We were cut from a different cloth in those days. In the 50's kids never wore shoes, at least not on the West Coast where I was raised. In those days, no one ever locked their doors. My mother never had a key to her house, even up until the day she died. She had a neighborhood "coffee clutch" every day. All of the neighborhood ladies would come over, sit at her kitchen table and discuss whatever moms discussed in those days.

My house was the hang-out house. I always had friends over, especially to dance. One night, my best friend, Tony came over with a bottle of Blue Nun Wine. Like a dumb shit, I thought it was cooking wine and it didn't contain any alcohol. I took to it like milk to a baby, it was mouthwatering. I chugged down the whole bottle all by myself in about three minutes. To make a long story longer, I wished someone would have warned me that going down was the easy part. The after effects were a son of a bitch. I vomited for three days straight and never drank again. If anything, I try to learn from my mistakes. It doesn't always work out that way, as you will see later when I discuss my second marriage.

At the age of sixteen, and with years of responsible work experience under my belt I was ready for the real world. At least, so I thought. I quit high school and got my first job as a carhop at Bob's Big Boy Restaurant. It was in Toluca Lake, California and during that time Bob's was where the "in crowd" hung out. On weekend nights, everyone would cruise Bob's in their 1930's, 1940s, and 1950s hot rods.

Geo's wife Thelma had also been a car hop at Bob's (Thelma and I had to make one last trip, just to get our pictures taken "in uniform" with the Original Bob's Big Boy.

Just how popular was this place? As of today, Jay Leno still drives one of his many classic cars through Bob's on weekend nights. Hey Jay! I'm waving at you. I eventually went back to high school, only I didn't graduate. I had taken a year off to work at Bob's, and I didn't have enough credits to graduate. Ergo, I have never been invited to any high school reunions. Maybe, if my memoir here is a success, I will be invited. Funny how fame tends to give you an in after you're ousted. Recently Geo's wife, Thelma, went with me because she had also been a carhop at Bob's Big Boy five decades before. Thelma was ninety years old, and I was seventy-seven years old at the time. I contacted the owner of Bobs and asked if we could buy a couple of Bob's Big Boy uniforms for old time sakes. He was kind enough to give us both uniforms with our own name tags. With our new uniforms and official name tags, Thelma and I played waitress for the day. We went to every table and introduced ourselves to everyone, as the "Oldest Living Bob's Big Boy Car Hops" left in the United States. We had the time of our lives.

CHAPTER THREE

My first real job after high school was working for a company that made airplane parts. The HR guy took a liking to me and trained me to work in every aspect of the office. I started in the mail room, and then he sent me to TWX school to become a TWX operator. I know what you are thinking ... but no, that isn't someone who makes Twix candy bars. For those of you that are too young to know what a TWX machine is, it is a machine that has an odd keyboard, similar to a typewriter keyboard but when you hit one or more of the keys at the same time, it punches out a kind of ticker tape. That tape goes into the TWX machine and sends messages over the wire to communicate with other TWX machines in other states. Sort of like the first computer. God, am I dating myself!!

I really liked it there and worked there on and off for many years. Since I had been trained in all aspects of the office, I filled in for people who called in sick or went on vacation. I spent a great deal of time in HR, because I loved to take tests. Every time a new test for an applicant came into HR, the director would call me in to take it first and critique it. I loved it.

I also worked at the front desk as a receptionist/PBX operator. In those days, the PBX was like the old-time telephone operator. You had a board with many holes in it in front of you. When a call came in to the company, you would answer it by plugging in one of the holes with a cable, and a metal prong at the end, to the board. To transfer that call to someone, you would take another wire plug and plug it into that person's hole on the board. It was sometimes hard to find the right hole when you had a lot of calls. Just think of Lily Tomlin for those of you who remember her comedy skits . . .

One ringy dingy, Two ringy dingy."

Of course, you had to use your perfect voice when answering calls. "Aeroquip, may I assist you?"

I was young and liked to walk through the shop back to the cafeteria and get whistled at. While there, they asked me to pose on the cover of their monthly magazine. I was so flattered. I still have a copy of that Magazine.

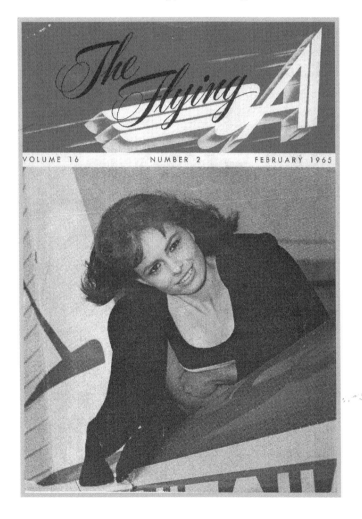

Shortly thereafter my stint at Aeroquip, I got married. I met him on a blind date that my mother arraigned. You can imagine my reaction when my mother told me that she wanted me to meet this very nice boy that worked with her. My initial reaction was, no way in hell, I am not having it. However, she persisted.

When I first spoke with him on the phone, I was not impressed. I heard this very slow southern drawl that pulled at my patience. Shit! I imagined someone with only three teeth in his mouth, and even those were decayed. No way was I going out with him. None the less, I was pressured into it.

On our first date, I sat way over next to the passenger door as if ready to toss myself out it needed. I was thinking to myself, he had better not try to kiss me. When he didn't, and he took me home, it sort of sealed the deal. The tables of resistance had turned and I had to have him. Actually, he was very handsome and also quite funny. We had a lot of fun together.

Within a few months, we ran off to Tijuana, Mexico to get married. When we got down there, we didn't know where to go to make it official. We went into the Catholic Church even though neither of us was catholic. His father was a Presbyterian minister and I was raised in a local Christian church. We couldn't find a priest, so we turned around and went home. Some months later, I discovered that I was pregnant, so we hurriedly planned a wedding. My grandmother made my wedding gown from my design. Obviously, I had no idea how to design a wedding dress but down the aisle we went. It was a real joke. He didn't have any family in town and I had literally thousands of family members in attendance.

You know how the groom's family usually sits on the right side of the church and the bride's family sits on the left? Well, my side was filled to standing room only and his side didn't have anyone on it. You would think that some of my family would sit on his side, especially the ones that were standing. But, oh no, that would have made too much sense, I guess.

They were sticking to their traditional ways. Finally, some of my friends did go over and sit on his side, but it was still beyond pathetic. When I came down the aisle and saw that, I felt so bad for him that I wanted to turn around and leave. But I was pregnant, so down the aisle I went. Our daughter was born six months later, (prematurely) dousing all hope of claiming a fake premature birth.

LOVE-ET' KAYPULLS

She grew up in some historic times. I remember when she was three years old President John F Kennedy was assassinated. That is one of those moments in time that you just never forget. I was vacuuming the house when the announcement came over the television set. I was so devastated, that I sat down on the floor and cried. My daughter became concerned and asked me why I was crying. I didn't believe in talking baby talk to children. I believed in talking to them honestly and in adult terminology. How else were they ever going to learn the English language properly?

"The President of the United States has just been assassinated," I said.

"Well, I didn't do it," she replied.

Out of the mouths of babes. I then, explained it to her in a little simpler way, using language she could more easily understand. My mother had been a stickler on grammar with me growing up, and I just didn't know any other way to talk.

Unfortunately, that marriage only lasted six years. I divorced him because he undermined my parenting skills. My daughter does not speak to me to this day. I think it began when she would ask me for cookies or candy just before dinner time, and I would explain to her that she could have it after dinner. Well, guess who would go in the other room and build a fort out of sheets and chairs and climb under there with her and feed her cookies and candy? Not me. It's a shame too, because he was a truly nice guy with a great sense of humor. I will forever love him.

My daughter never forgave me for divorcing him and she was too young for me to explain the circumstances to her. My life with my daughter was a downhill battle for many years. I know I wasn't a very good mother, but I tried. After all, I was only eighteen-years old when she was born. The only parenting skills I acquired were learned from my mother. I wish I had a chance to do it over, but of course I don't.

To support my daughter after the divorce, I got a job as a cocktail waitress. At the time, it paid the best money I was able to make, but I hated it. I was a non-drinker, due to getting accidentally drunk at sixteen. My mother permitted my sister and I to drink in moderation as teenagers, so we never felt the need to drink alcohol regularly, or away from home. Working as a cocktail waitress only heightened my distain for over consumption.

In order to work, I had to hire live-in babysitters. I could not get a regular one because I lived out in the boondocks. I realized that this was a crucial decision and there was no way I was going to find someone who was as cheap and responsible as I was. I tried to screen them as well as I knew how, which apparently wasn't very good.

Some friends lived next door to me. One day my friend came over. "Is your daughter, all right?" she asked.

I didn't know why she was asking, so I pressed her for an explanation. "Well," she hesitated, "Last night your babysitter came over to my house. She was drunk and asked us if we would drive her to the liquor store to buy more booze."

"Ok, and …" I pressed. "My husband did it for her," she admitted.

I could not even believe I was hearing this. They left my tiny daughter home alone and drove her to buy booze. Then let her go back in my house to continuing watching my child. She then had the gall to tell me they were so worried about my daughter all night that they could barely sleep. My mouth dropped to the floor, and it was all I could do to keep from beating the shit out of her.

"I hope it didn't inconvenience you too much," I said between gritted teeth. "I know you had to leave your nice warm home to take that drunk down to get more booze! Why didn't you call me at work? I gave you the phone number in case of an emergency?"

"Oh, we didn't want to bother you at work," she said. "But just so you know, we were worried sick all night."

I handed her five dollars to reimburse her for their gas. She was too stupid to even get my intended sarcasm. Needless to say, I never spoke to either of them again. I would have beaten the shit out of both them, but he was a big mucky- muck and would certainly have had me arrested. I didn't have enough sense to call the police and have them arrested like I should have.

CHAPTER FOUR

Shortly thereafter the "wanting to kill my baby sitter and neighbor's incident" someone cut the top on my convertible. I called the police to make a police report. Enter husband number two. It was love at first sight for both of us, or so I thought. All I can tell you is that he was gorgeous.

When he arrived at my house, I wasn't wearing any make-up. So, every few minutes I would excuse myself, run into the other room and put on an eyebrow. Then another one and little by little I appeared in full make-up. I thought I was being very clever, but it was all he could do to keep from bursting out laughing at me. It was just a routine report call, but he ended up staying for hours.

Finally, after I had made a complete fool of myself, he asked me if I would go out with him. We were sitting at the kitchen table, and I stood up, slid my body across the table. "I thought you would never ask," I smiled.

We married three days later and remained married for forty years. Sounds like a fairy tale love story, right? Wrong! That was the biggest mistake of my life. He was a horrible womanizer our entire marriage.

The frustrations made me want to shoot or choke the living hell out of him. It was then that I finally decided to pursue my career in law enforcement. Go figure.

At first, I applied to The Los Angeles Police Department, but they rejected me. They didn't have any policewomen on their department, at that time. I was devastated. But all was not lost. Remember my friend Geo? He told me to try the Los Angeles County Sheriff's Department. I did, and they rejected me too.

Instead of getting frustrated I got more determined. Oh no, I'm not having any of this shit! I really wanted to become a policewoman more than anything. Some girls want to be great singers; others want to be movie stars. I just wanted to become a policewoman, and I was determined that nothing would stop me. I even considered that perhaps something deeply rooted in me was holding me back. What if there was something that I might not have even been aware of, something from my past?

At one point, when I was still a teen, I was trying to sort out my life. Since I was having problems getting along with my mother, I went to a psychiatrist to see if I could figure her out. She, of course, refused to go with me because there wasn't anything wrong with her. So, I went on my own and paid for it with my babysitting money. That was a waste of money because I was never able to figure her out at any cost. One day, I came right out and asked her why she didn't like me. Her response floored me. "I could tell by the look on your face when you were born that you were smarter than me," she said. "I also knew that you would cause me nothing but grief."

I know what you are thinking. Trust me, I was thinking the same thing. How can a newborn infant have that kind of a look on her face? At any rate, the psychiatrist wrote something very ambiguous down in my chart. That brings us full circle back to my endeavor to become a policewoman.

The Sheriff's Department requested my medical history. Sure enough, that ambiguous remark came to their attention. Since they didn't know what it meant, they disqualified me. Bullshit! Not a second time. Not without a fight!

I took the paperwork to a new psychiatrist for his interpretation of it. He assured me that the language in it was only a wastebasket term that meant nothing. Just a big word some psychiatrists like to throw out there. He wrote me a new letter of explanation that would satisfy the sheriff's department. After that, he asked me out on a date. What a horn dog he was.

Anyway, horn dog or not, it did satisfy the department. The next obstacle was to pass the physical test. I had already aced the written exam, so all I had to do was bluff my way through the physical test. I knew I could pass the physical agility portion hands down. However, you see, I was only five-feet, two inches tall and weighed one hundred ten pounds. The requirements were five-feet, three inches and one hundred sixteen pounds. Now why should I let a little thing like that deter me?

For a month before the physical, I ate bananas and cream by the crate. Along with that, I also devoured everything I could get my hands on that would fatten me up. I worked out as much as possible to ace the physical agility test. I ran every day to get in shape. My husband tried to run with me, but he pooped out after about a half block. So much for his back up! Now it was time for the physical.

For a week before the test, I went to a chiropractor every day for several hours having him pop my back and try to stretch my height. Sounds ridiculous, right? Not for me. On the day of my physical, I again went to the chiropractor and had him do his magic. This time, my husband drove me to the physical test while I was lying on my back in the rear of his van. When we got inside, the tester put a piece of paper under my heels so I couldn't try to cheat, while she pulled on the paper. Not a problem for me. I just mentally started at my ankles, worked the way up my body all the way to the top of my head and mentally stretched my entire body until I reached five-feet, three inches. I have never been that tall since and never needed to be. When it came to the weight, the best I could come up with was one hundred twelve pounds. They gave me six months to gain the weight. I never did and they never checked. Instead, I went back down to my original weight. Fifty years later, I've gained it back, plus some. After all the tests and determination, one day I got the notice to show up at the academy. I had been hired! I guess sticking to your goals will pay off if you don't give up. It is amazing what you can accomplish if you just set your mind to it and use a little imagination. Now the party was about to start.

CHAPTER FIVE

I was notified to report for duty, and it finally sunk in that this was really happening. They quickly swore me in and sent me to Sybil Brand Institute for Women to work as an off the street deputy. Off the street, identifies you as someone who has not yet gone through the Sheriff's Academy. Sybil Brand was named after a philanthropist of that time. Ms. Brand was very interested in the rehabilitation of women inmates and liked to host shows for the girls in our auditorium that doubled as a theatre stage. I helped to produce several shows there myself. Sybil Brand was the only women's correctional facility at that time.

Built in 1963, it had a capacity for nine hundred women, but at its peak we had twenty-eight hundred incarcerated there. When Sybil Brand closed in 1997, the inmates were transferred to the Twin Towers Building in downtown Los Angeles. The county may renovate it and reopen it as a prison. In the meantime, it offers modern-looking prison rooms that included cafeterias, hallways, recreation areas, visiting room infirmaries, and cells from solitary confinement to dormitories for film crews. As a women's prison, the walls were painted pink, which is usually painted over during filming. Productions film there at a rate of two to three times per month. The Johnny Depp film "Blow," a true story about cocaine dealers, spent five weeks shooting all over the prison. Other productions include: "Arrest and Trial," "Gangland," "The X Files," "America's Most Wanted," and "Desperate Housewives. "The first thing I learned was that the inmates are much smarter than the deputies. They have street smarts and the deputies don't. For the most part, the deputies have led a very straight life and have never been subjected to the hard knocks of the streets. The inmates can con you so fast with such a straight face that it would blow your mind. My first assignment was to work the cell blocks for newly arrested inmates. That meant that they could be in for murder, a simple drunk charge, or traffic violation. At Sybil Brand, the cell blocks were back to back. Twelve were on one side and twelve were on the other. There was an extended plumbing corridor separating the two sides. Each cell had bars on it, not doors. Outside the cell was a walkway separated by another set of bars. That allowed inmates to be let out of their cells individually to go to court, to see their attorney, or go to the infirmary.

If an inmate had to leave her cell to go to one of these places, it was my job to let her out and see to it that she got to her destination. At first, I was frightened. What if they jumped me when I let them out? Well, I soon found out. The fight was on. It's amazing how well you can fight when you really have to, even if you have never had a fight in your life. Remember, at this time I had not had any training, so I pretty much had to play it by ear.

Each cell housed two women, but we were overcrowded, so we had to put a third woman on the floor under the bottom bunk. There were two sets of bars. One set of the bars enclosed the cell, the other set divided the cell from the outer area. It was the deputy's job to walk down the aisle between the cells and the outer set of bars every twenty minutes. These rounds were made to ensure that they hadn't hung themselves.

Sometimes this could be a problem. Many of them would save up their coffee cups and either urinate or defecate in them, sometimes both. Often, they would throw the contents on you. You had to be very quick on your feet and have eyes in the back of your head. I never got hit, but it was not for the lack of their trying.

My favorite place to work was the Ding Tank. We were not very politically correct at that time, referring to the mentally disturbed inmates as dings. I loved them! I was among my own kind. They were such poor lost souls, and my heart went out to them. It was amazing what they they would say and do.

One woman kept asking me to get her false teeth out of her paisley purse. So, I made several trips to the property room to go through her property. I could never find them in spite of her constant insistence that they were there. Finally, I returned to discover that she was wearing her false teeth. "So where did you get them," I asked after being surprised that she had them.

"Out of my paisley purse," she said, lifting up her dress exposing her vagina.

Another woman came in insisting that she was Priscilla Presley, Elvis's wife. She kept calling out to him all night long, disturbing the other inmates. Her calling out for him wasn't half as bad as when she would sing to him at the top of her lungs. Completely off key, of course. All in all, I look back at those days fondly. One thing is for certain, I will never forget those women.

CHAPTER SIX

Five months after my virgin initiation in the force, I was transferred to the Sheriffs Training Academy. All I can say is, it was about time. My class was #132 and I had a woman drill instructor. She was a beautiful young woman with red hair named, Beth Dickenson. Unfortunately, she died in 2017 and will never see this book or know how much I loved and respected her. There is a picture in the book of me yelling at her. (We had to yell everything.) She was looking at the serial number on the butt of my gun and told me to recite it.

One hundred and eighty-six people started the class. There were thirty-two women and one hundred and fifty-four men. Only one hundred and six graduated. Thirty-one women and seventy-five men made it to the other side.

No one but me thought the academy was a fun place. They were hard on you all of the time. It was similar to the old boot camp days. Where you were being yelled at constantly, and a drill instructor was always inches away from your face, yelling at you to recite something. Usually something you didn't know anything about. It was all a mental game because it was their job to weed out the weak as well as the people with short fuses. They didn't want any hot heads in the department.

I was a real trouper and so were all of the other girls. We really stuck together, and it was fun. When the drill instructors yelled at the top of their lungs, trying to get you to drop out, it was all I could do to keep from laughing. Actually, I did laugh on several occasions and that did not go over well with them.

The drill staff had a warped sense of humor. Of course, it was their job to make your life so miserable until you just couldn't hang in any longer and eventually would quit. That was the entire point. If you couldn't handle yourself under pressure, The Department didn't want you. A policeman's job is extremely stressful and so The Department wants to weed out the week and the hotheads, as soon as possible. One of their torture techniques, was a game we all remember fondly, called "Quickie Changie." We had two sets of uniforms. Our class A uniform, and our Physical Training clothes. Our Class A uniform was the uniform you see deputies wearing out in patrol. Our Physical Training clothes were the ones we wore when we were doing our exorcizes. Running, sit ups, pull ups, etc. Usually, at some point after we had a very strenuous training session and couldn't wait to go back into the classroom and sit down to catch our breath, One of the DI's, (drill instructors) would yell out, just as we sat down to rest for a second, "Quickie Changie!" Oh no!! Not the dreaded "Quickie Changie!" We were immediately given the command that we had exactly 5 minutes to change out of our P.T. gear and into our Class A Uniforms. We would all jump up, run to our locker room and take off all of our clothes hang them up and redress into our Class A uniforms. We could hear the Training Officers counting down the time. My class had 32 women in it. The Department hadn't made any allowances for us to have a locker room area. All we had was a woman's restroom, where they had thrown in a handful of lockers. So, there we were. 32 women pushing and shoving against one another, trying to get one set of clothes off and another set of clothes on. What we didn't know, was the DI's would stand outside of our little bathroom area and listen to EVERYTHING we said. "Time's up cadets." Yelled a D.I. Out we all scrambled back into the classroom and into our seats. No sooner had we sat down, another D.I. would yell, "Well, apparently that was too easy. So, now, you only have 4 minutes to change back into your P.T. gear and then back into your seats."

The sound of the chairs screeching on the gymnasium floor and several hundred men and woman madly running back toward their locker rooms was almost deafening! Needless to say, this little torturous game went on for what seemed like an eternity. Each time the completion time got shorter and shorter. After about the 4th or 5th time, the Drill Instructors decided that some of us had to be cheating! NOW, the fun really begins!! So, they started yelling out questions! "How many of you are wearing your P.T. socks over your Class A socks?" A few hands went up. "How many of you did not change out of your P.T. t-shirt and into your Class A t-shirt?" A few more hands went up. One of the girls in my platoon, although she was a sweetheart and a really nice girl, I could tell she had led a very sheltered life. She sat right in front of me. One of the DI's yelled out, "How many of you are not wearing your Jock Strap?" She very slowly raised her hand. I could tell she didn't have a clue as to what a Jock Strap was, and I just couldn't control my laughter one more second! I burst out hysterically laughing and before I knew what hit me, about eight Drill Instructors surrounded me, each yelling at the top of their lungs, and each asking me a different question! Answering eight different questions at the top of my lungs, all at the same time, was an impossible feat. By now, my laughter had built up to absolute hysteria. I could no longer control myself. Finally, one of the Drill Instructors realized the futility of me ever regaining my composure and screamed at me to get out of the classroom and run around the outside parking lot until I had regained my control. He didn't have to tell me twice! I popped up out of my seat and headed for the parking lot, laughing hysterically all of the way. I ran out of the c   the parking lot. All of the time, I played the over in my head. Finally, a Drill Instructor class took notice of me and as he approached me, he was yelling, "Recruit! Just what do you think is so funny?" Again, in my head, I saw Jackie raising her hand for not wearing her Jock Strap. Hysteria overtook me and by now I was screaming in laughter. "Get running cadet, and don't stop running until you can tell me what you are laughing at!" Off I went! Every time I came around the parking lot there was at least one more Drill Instructor standing there to ask me the question. "What are you laughing at?" Eventually, I didn't even stop. I just looked at them as I ran by and laughed even harder. My stomach hadn't hurt that bad since childbirth, but I just couldn't stop. Finally, after almost everyone had gone home, someone took pity on me and just yelled at me to get out of their parking lot and go home. I know for a fact that I laughed all of the way home and couldn't even repeat the story to my husband. Even today, I'm afraid to even let myself think of it. I loved the academy and all of it's torture. If I weren't so damn old, I would do it all again in a heartbeat.

I missed a lot of classroom work because I was running around the parking lot day after day, laughing my ass off. A funny thing, a girl that I worked with at Aeroquip was also in my class. Her name was Betty Sanders. She too has passed on and will never see my book. She also made it through the academy, and we worked together for years. She never understood why I was a glutton for punishment. Or why I thought everything was so funny. I guess it is

...st part of my personality. I love to laugh and make other people laugh.

Now back to the academy. Class work was a bitch. We had to print everything, and I was raised to use cursive writing. I still can't print worth a damn, and now I hear that they don't even teach cursive writing anymore. The Sheriff's Academy was one of the best times of my life. Although most days were amazing, I did get secretly pissed once. We had a physical agility exam, and I knew I was going to ace it. They assigned each of us a designated person to count our repetitions. Guess who was assigned to count my repetitions? You guessed it. Little miss I'm not wearing my jock strap! I was counting mine in my head and she was counting mine, apparently on her fingers. Well she miscounted mine. Oh, she didn't just miscount by a little, but by a lot! Due to this error, I came in second instead of first. It was only a game. No big deal. I got over it instantly. And, if you believe that, I have some swamp land for sale. Eventually, she became one of my dearest friends. Our graduation however was a big deal. My whole family attended it. What a spectacle we were!

My family consists of many aunts, uncles, and even more cousins. I love my family, and they are so supportive. Even my ex-husband was there. I told you he was a great guy. After graduation, I was reassigned back to Sybil Brand. Yes, back to the shit throwing, the stench, and the ratchet rat race. All the fun of a chaotic carnival was waiting for me to join in the madness.

Shortly after I returned to the jail, the Charlie Manson Girls were brought in there. What a site they were. Filthy, dirty, covered with lice, and each giggling and playing with each other's long, mangy hair like insane witches. We couldn't put them in the cell blocks with the other inmates because they were so lice-infested. We had to segregate them in the day room. This was a large room with many stationary tables and chairs used by the cellblock inmates to watch TV and read. It took us forever to delouse them because of their long hair. So, they stayed in there day after day playing and watching TV.

They had just brutally murdered several people, but you never would have guessed it by the way they were acting. Actually, they weren't brought in on murder charges, at all. They were brought in on some insignificant charge. I think it was for trespassing or something like that. We, along with the rest of the world, had no clue what they had done. We probably never would have even known about it if one of them, Susan Atkins, booked in as Sadie Glutz hadn't bragged to another inmate months later about what they had done.

Manson could have easily gotten out and ordered even more brutal murders if she hadn't talked.

One thing was undeniable. They loved Charlie Manson from his crazy head to his stubby toes. That one conversation exposed the Manson family otherwise we may never have caught them.

When they were all re-arrested for murder and the news media found out, the shit really hit the fan. That fiasco went on for years, with them shaving their heads and cutting swastikas in their foreheads. They were a news media blitz for years. Susan Atkins once told me that she had a son by Charlie Manson and she said she named him, Zazoozeeseesefree Zadfrack Glutz. I don't know if that was true or not, but I do know that she did give birth to a son. Whether he was actually Charlie Manson's son, I am not sure. Those girls lived in a free love society with Charlie Manson and had many lovers. I am certain that child was adopted out somewhere and his identity will never be known to him. There is a distinctive possibility that not even to the adoptive parents know of that kid's dark history. All I know is, that I sure hope there isn't another Charlie Manson out there somewhere.

Soon, I was transferred to the dormitories and assigned to three of them. Each dormitory slept eighty women. If my math is correct, that equates to two hundred and forty inmates that I was supervising. Keep in mind one thing here, these dorms weren't locked. The inmates had full access to leave to go to their work assignments. The deputies were, however, locked in for their own safety. We were locked in a guard station so we could oversee everyone, but we were not at risk.

The dorms were separated from the cell blocks by a corridor locked gate. At meal times, it was my job to let all of the inmates out into the hall to line up against the wall. They would have to travel across to the cellblock side and up the long dark ramp to the second floor where the cafeteria was. They had to line up on the far wall and very quietly walk to the cafeteria. The inmates weren't allowed to speak or make any noise. During that time period, the song My Cherie Amor was very popular. They played music in the halls on the way to meals. The girls couldn't help themselves from singing it on the way to chow and I didn't have the heart to stop them. I am so lucky that I wasn't fired for allowing them to break the rules. Eventually,

I was noticed by the classification lieutenant, and offered a job working for her. At first, I was reluctant to leave, but she reminded me that it was a promotion, so how could I refuse?

That meant that my new job was to go back to the cell blocks and interview all newly sentenced women inmates to determine what job assignments they were best suited for. My time in HR at Aeroquip really helped out. The prison had several jobs at which to work. Remember, a prison is a little city within a city. We have a kitchen, dining room, and sewing room. We made our own prison uniforms as well as other items. We also had a laundry room, janitorial work, and even a beauty shop. For the honor inmates we had an outside activities area. There they can make pottery, quilting, toys (to give to the needy or sell to the public), and lots of other hand crafts. The inmates in this minimum-security side were kept busy. If you have ever seen the Netflix show Orange is the New Black, that is somewhat how our honor dorms looked like. The only difference is that our cubicles were much smaller and only housed one inmate.

Once, I accidentally told my lieutenant that I had an ex-boyfriend named Bill. From that day forward, she insisted on calling my husband Bill, even to him, when he would call me at work. She called me Minnie Mouse, because I had skinny legs and big feet. She even went so far as to have a ceramic doll, resembling Minnie Mouse, dressed in a sheriff uniform made and presented it to me. I still have it on a shelf in my bedroom where I keep all of my favorite memorabilia. I worked at classification the rest of my career at Sybil Brand. I was loaned out, to many other units to work for short periods of time but I didn't mind that at all. In fact, I loved it; working in other departments broke up the monotony.

My first outside assignment was to work at Vice. In those days massage parlors were a booming business. We knew that they were really prostitution houses but we could never catch the owners. Our vice guys were able to go in and catch the girls for offering sex for money. The owners always claimed they didn't know anything about it. That is where I came into the picture. It was my job to pose as a prospective massage therapist/hooker and somehow get the owners to come right out and say that they wanted me to commit prostitution. It wasn't that easy. They were very careful of what they said and to whom they said it to, in order not to incriminate themselves. It was like a cat and mouse game or a well- choreographed dance that we did over and over.

I would do my best to get them to say that they wanted me to commit prostitution and they would do their best not to outright say it. It was almost comical. It's a good thing I'm perseverant and have a good sense of humor or I would have gotten frustrated. Eventually, my relaxed demeanor and perseverance paid off. I was always able to get them to admit to whatever I wanted them to on a secretly hidden tape recorder I was wearing. We never arrested them immediately; we waited until we had all of the owners on tape and then made a large arrest closing them all down at the same time. Had we arrested them each time they admitted they were operating whore houses, word would get around to the other massage parlors, and we wouldn't get any more information, so, we waited until we got all of the information on all of them, and then in one fell swoop, we arrested all of them in the same day.

Once, I was in a second-floor room, interviewing a group of around five men suspected of running a house of prostitution. Three of the men had a cat-of nine-tails, protruding from their rear pockets. I must admit, that time, I was frightened. Since they were blocking the only exit door, I determined that in case of an emergency escape, I would have to jump out the second-story plate glass window. Fortunately for me, it didn't occur. Instead, they told me that they wanted to fly me to Hawaii, to run one of their massage parlors/whore houses and they wanted me to leave for Hawaii that afternoon. I agreed, and told them I had to run downstairs to get my traveling clothes out of my boyfriends' car. It seemed logical to them, so I scurried downstairs and ran for a few blocks looking for my backup. It is a misconception to the general public that your backup people are always a step away. Well, I'm here to tell you, that is a bunch of malarkey. I worked a lot of undercover assignments in my career, and I can honestly say that not ONCE was my backup ever waiting for me, or even had a clue where I was. Another misnomer was that the undercover wire I wore ever worked. Not once did we get anything on tape. Our equipment was so antiquated, we should have just thrown it away. But we had to at least pretend that all of these conversations I was having with these dirtbags was all on tape and could be played for the jury in court.

That meant that I had to write down the conversations by memory each time I left a location. My backup couldn't even hear my conversations. I had a great memory and it was never a problem for me, but in court, that was a different story. When the defense attorneys discovered that we didn't have anything on tape, they went for my throat!

The defense attorneys would consistently try to test my memory to see if I really could recall conversations well after the fact. It was another cat and mouse game to me. They tried every trick in the book to cross me up and prove I couldn't remember all of those conversations. But I just sat back and smiled at them and answered all of their ridiculous questions as fast as they threw them at me. One of the defense attorneys was so stupid that he tried to get me to tell him what I was wearing the previous Tuesday in court. What a stupid question to ask a woman. Of course, she remembers everything she wore last week, down to every detail, so she doesn't duplicate it this week. I was able to tell them down to the jewelry and perfume. Then the fool asked me what he was wearing last Tuesday. Well, I knew for sure that he didn't remember so I said, "The same suit you wore on Friday." The courtroom erupted in uproarious laughter and it took the judge almost five minutes to get order in the court. In the meantime, that defense attorney was running around the courtroom insisting that it wasn't true, but too late. The damage had been done. I had humiliated him in front of all of his peers. After all of the trials were over, the prosecution attorney approached me and told me I was the best prosecution witness he had ever had. It was very flattering, but I couldn't take it to the bank.

Next, I was sent to work credit card fraud. I didn't like that very much. The deputy in charge was the *DEPUTY IN CHARGE.* I really never got a chance to show my stuff, whatever that was. I don't know why I was even there. Maybe he just needed someone to carry the wire. Anyway, I didn't find it very challenging or rewarding. After that, I went to narcotics.

I didn't know diddly shit about narcotics and no one ever taught me. I was out of my element. We would go to these drug dealers' houses and sit around and try out the merchandise. WTF? I was able to move the cocaine around and make it look like I had snorted it and pinch the marijuana cigarette end so when I took a big puff, I didn't get any. The truth of it was, I don't think my partners did the same pretend tricks. That was disheartening.

I also was able to go to elementary schools and talk to the kids about the dangers of taking drugs. On many occasions, I was requested to come to the classroom and talk about women deputy sheriffs and what we do. The boys were especially interested to know if I knew any special holds or take down measures. They always loved it when I would call them up to the front of the class and demonstrate the holds on them. I showed them how to hold someone's hand and put their elbow in the crook of your own elbow, bend that person's middle finger back, while pushing the arm into the crook of their own elbow and forcing them to go wherever they were led. I'm certain the teachers hated it after I left the class and recess came and the boys would run outside and put each other in these holds all through recess. I received about fifty letters from the kids, telling me how much they liked my class and telling me how pretty I was. I have kept those letters as well. Periodically, I take them out of the box, just to remember that was all the kids got out of my elaborate speeches. They could just as easily have told me that I was a lousy speaker and ugly as hell. I'm grateful for that at least.

One day I came home and my husband told me that the sheriff's department was implementing a new pilot program. They were going to send women out into patrol and it would be a good opportunity for me. Of course, I immediately applied.

There were only hundreds of women deputies applying, so why should that be a problem for me? I had overcome obstacles before so why should this one be any different? I have always been pretty light on my feet, so I was pretty certain I could deliver a descent interview. The interviewers were mostly patrol sergeants, and for the most part they wanted to know how fast you could respond sensibly in a rapid manner. Then, one of them asked me what was the grossest thing I had ever seen. I told them about the mentally disturbed woman at the jail that had chewed her own nipples off. Then, after they were sewn back on, she chewed them off again. That one even grossed them out.

I got the job.

CHAPTER SEVEN

When it came down to it, a total of just twenty women were selected to go back to the academy through a special never before patrol school. We all worked our asses off. One thing was clear from the very start; every one of us wanted that job. Little did we know at the time, they were only going to select twelve of us to actually go to patrol.

As for the others, they would have to wait to see if the program was successful before they were allowed to go out. I was one of the ones selected. There were a lot of tears when the list was read and a lot of disappointment. The good news was, the program was a success and after one year, the other girls were also sent out to patrol.

At the Patrol School, we were taught many neat things. We were given instruction on how to drive a police car in pursuit. But it gets even better. We were taught how to do this backwards and on wet slippery roads. They set up orange cones a few feet apart going from one lane to another and in all kinds of crazy ways. Then we had to drive backwards through the cones at thirty-five miles an hour on a timed course.

We also learned how to whip a U-turn on a dime. Then the instructors taught us how to drive as fast as we could backwards. We were taught how to change lanes with only enough room for our cars to go through and that was a thrill of its own. Damn, it was exciting! All of that training really came in handy for me later as you will soon learn.

We were put through rigorous physical training as well. I am so grateful for that. Each day was a learning adventure and I looked forward to each one. All in all, Patrol School was another one of the best times of my life.

CHAPTER EIGHT

There were a lot of stations to be assigned to but all of them were not equal. Another girl and I were lucky enough to be sent to the Old West Hollywood Station. This station was located at 720 San Vicente Blvd. in West Hollywood, California. Her name was Carole Freeman and she was a real go-getter. She was promoted through the ranks very quickly and eventually retired as a Chief. West Hollywood Station was only a hop stitch and a jump over a mountain to my house, so I felt pretty lucky. My travel time over the mountain was only about thirty-five minutes.

My husband had taken me out car hunting and he wanted me to buy a Mercedes. While we were driving down the street, I saw this cute, tiny, little orange, two-cylinder, four-speed manual transmission. It was a 1972 Honda Z600 car, parked on the sidewalk, and I just had to have it. He never forgave me. It was only thirty-five hundred dollars out the door. That included radio, heater, license and registration. I decided that since it was parked on the sidewalk, when I first saw it that is where I should drive it. I loved that car. It was me. In fact, I kept that car until there wasn't anything left of it. Honda was only able to import that car that one year because it couldn't pass smog control. But since it was grandfathered in, I didn't have to worry about it.

Do any of you remember the big gas shortage of 1973? Well, I do, and it was a walk in the park for me. That car got fifty-miles to the gallon and in those days, that was unheard of. People were unable to buy gas anywhere. It was a madhouse. Cars lined up for blocks trying to get into a gas station, only to find out when they got to the front of the line, the station had run out of gas. What a crazy time that was, but not for me. I just drove to the gas station on the sidewalk until I was first in line. Yes, I'm aware that was a pretty dirty trick on my part. Am I the only one in the world who would do that if they knew they could get away with it without any consequences? I don't think so.

On my very first day of patrol, I was instructed to be there at O-dark thirty. For those of you who don't know, what actual time that is, there isn't any rule about it, it was just pretty darn early. So, I arrived at 6 AM. When I got there the watch sergeant told me that my shift didn't start until three o'clock PM. Rather than send me home to get some sleep, he decided it would be a good idea to take me out himself and show me the area. What he failed to tell me was that I was assigned to a ten- four shift. That meant that on my first shift, I would clock in at two-forty-five PM and work ten hours before going home. On my second day, I was scheduled to work a double ten-hour shift. Coming in at 2:45 PM and going home at 11:00 AM the next morning. On my next shift, I was to arrive at 1:00 AM and work until 11 AM the following morning. That was supposed to give me three days off, but since I had to sleep for a full eight hours to catch up, it really didn't give me three days.

I didn't care. I had broken the glass ceiling for women in patrol so I was opened to anything. I was now officially one of the first women to ever work in a patrol car in the United States. I couldn't have been happier if I had walked on the moon. My husband was certainly sorry that he had suggested it to me. He worked for the Los Angeles City Police Department for years. They had never heard of a schedule like that and certainly not overtime.

On my first shift I was assigned to work with a married deputy. His wife called the station Captain and told him that if he allowed her husband to work with a woman, she would divorce him. So, the captain assigned me to work with a bachelor. His name was Gary Huffman and I am proud to say, he is one of the most dedicated, hardworking, no-nonsense people I have ever known.

Gary & I at WHD   Gary & I yrs. later

Gary did love overtime however and this was much to my husband's dismay. Since I had arrived at O-dark thirty, my shift didn't start until 2:45 PM, Gary wanted to stop and arrest as many bad guys as possible. This meant that I didn't get off work until 8:00 AM the next day. When I got home, my jealous husband was furious. I really didn't need that shit. The next shift I only worked twenty-four hours instead of twenty-six from the night before. When I got home, he laid into me.

"Why did you have to work twenty-six hours on your first day on the job and only twenty-four hours on your second day, he said in his most sarcastic voice?"

I really didn't like his innuendos, and I was pissed. "Because on my first day at work I had to fuck every guy at the station," I yelled. "And on my second day, I only had to fuck the good ones and I don't know how many I'm going to have to fuck tonight!"

With that, he threw my bed pillow on the couch and slammed the bedroom door. Now, I know I could have handled it better, but I was tired and really pissed off. I really resented his innuendos. I guess if you are an unfaithful asshole, you assume that everyone else is also. The rest of my time in patrol didn't go much better, but we survived.

It is customary when you work with a radio car partner for the first time, to discuss possible situations that may arise, and how to respond to them for the safety of both you and your partner.

On our first shift together, I knew Gary was going to be concerned about my safety if anything unforeseen occurred. The first thing I did was address the issue before it became one.

"Okay," I said. "Here is the plan. If we get in trouble out there, I'm going to rip open my blouse, exposing my 44DD breasts, and while the bad guys are too busy being shocked and looking at my boobs, you get the draw on them."

This broke the ice. Gary and I got along famously after that. I was a few years older than him, so he wasn't interested in me romantically. Instead, we just had a blast.

Come to think of it, very few deputies ever did hit on me, and when they did, in order not to hurt their feelings, or, offend them, I would always say the same thing.

"I'm flattered! I'd love to sleep with you, however, I think you should be aware of something beforehand. I am married to an angry eight-foot gorilla stuffed into a six-foot man's body. If you don't mind me being the very last piece of ass you'll ever have, let's do it!" It didn't take more than a split second for them to make their decision. They thanked me very much and it was never brought up again.

We made lots of great arrests and even found time for play. The sheriff had also implemented another new program called "Team Policing." That meant that not only did we do patrol work, but we were also required to go into the detective bureau and do the detective follow up on our own cases. I loved working in the detective bureau. The guys in there were very laid back and fun. One of the detectives reminded me the other day about an incident that happened to him in DB. His name is Paul Forester. He was one of the funniest guys I've ever met. He also wore the most delicious men's cologne I've ever smelled. Every time he came to work with a new fragrance, I immediately bought some for my husband, Sam.

Speaking of Paul, here is one of his favorite stories, he likes to tell.

By Paul Forster
Some names were omitted intentionally.

While working the Night Car at West Hollywood DB, in 1974 several of us (4) were sitting in the Detective

Bureau Office conducting "house cleaning activities". Such as reading Teletypes and discussing how to assist the day Detectives in their assignment requests, etc. As UCLA was playing New Mexico for the NCAA March Madness Championship that night, one of the Detectives obtained (liberated) a Television from the evidence room and plugged it in the DB and we were watching the game.

The night Station Watch Commander came into the DB Office and observed us watching the game. His desires were immediately obvious, and he ordered us to return the TV to the Evidence Locker and get out on the street to further support the Patrol Deputies, which is what we were supposed to be doing, in his mind.

One of the senior Detectives immediately called the DB Lieutenant, at home, and advised him of what had transpired. Being a level-headed individual, he advises the caller not to worry about it and to just go out into the field.

My Partner, Denny Rusler (Rip Denny) left the station and proceeded West Bound on Santa Monica Blvd. Denny was driving and I was riding shotgun. As we passed an all-night grocery store Denny said to me "Hey I just saw someone come running out of the store carrying a bag and pulling a wig off of his head.

We immediately turned around and proceeded in the direction of the location where Denny saw the individual running. As we started up the street, we observed a 1970 Cadillac pulling away from the curb heading toward Fountain Ave.

We obtained the vehicle license plate number. At the corner of Fountain and, I forgot the other name of the street, the vehicle turned right or west and Denny hit them with the spotlight and I advised the Radio Room of our observation and the vehicle took off, going Eastbound on Fountain.

We proceeded to follow them and I advised on the radio that we were in pursuit of two Robbery suspects in a yellow, with a black vinyl top, Cadillac, proceeding West Bound on Fountain. As we proceeded to follow the vehicle at a very high rate of speed, I noticed several Radio Cars going West Bound in the opposite direction.

As luck would have it, I was advising via Radio Room that we were going West Bound, when in fact we were going Eastbound, and the Radio room was echoing what we were telling them.

The Cadillac made a right turn on Poinsettia Drive, which immediately splits into West and East Poinsettia drive.

The crooks went East and Denny and I went West. Fortunately, the crooks in the Cadillac passed a LAPD unit, that was looking for an address, as they had received a call that was out of there area.

The crooks bailed out of the Cadillac in the middle of the block and began running in opposite directions, and were followed by the LAPD unit, and two of the LASD Radio Car personnel.

One of the citizens called the station and advised that there was someone lying in his driveway, who had knocked on his back door and when he opened it the individual was pointing a 45-semi auto pistol at him. The citizen noted that there was no magazine in the pistol and kicked the crook in the chest.

The LASD radio car immediately apprehended the passed-out suspect and his unloaded pistol while the LAPD Unit apprehended the other individual and recovered the money and the wig.

The suspects were booked at West Hollywood station, and all the money was recovered, and UCLA won the Basketball Game to become National Champs….

Lovette continues …………….

I wanted to make certain that I was well received at the station by the other deputies, so I always brought in, goodie bags. They were full of food to hand out during our shift. Since, one of our shifts was an early morning shift and The Deliverance was a hot movie at the time, Gary and I would drive through residential areas with Dueling Banjos blaring loudly on our outside speakers. We would drive fast so that no one would discover it was a patrol car making all of the noise. I wish that I hadn't waited so long to start writing this book, because I have forgotten so much of it. I'm seventy-seven years old now, and this occurred back in 1972, when I was only thirty-one-years-old. Time really does fly.

Since I was only five-foot two-inches tall and one hundred and ten pounds, whenever another deputy received a burglary call and he needed to climb in a second-story window, he would always call me over to do it. I could fit through easily and was not cumbered down with a gun belt. He would pull his car up close to the window and climb on top of the car. Then I would shimmy up his back and straddle his shoulders. Then, just before I climbed in the window, I would very calmly say, "Damn! It's times like this when I wish I had worn underwear." Their flashlights would go on and their neck would snapback, desperately trying to look up my mini skirt. Gary never got tired of my joke and laughed at it every time.

Early on, at West Hollywood, we received a burglary call. A woman reported that a man had tried to break into her home and he had run into the back yard. We knew the guy wasn't still in her backyard, so we split up. I jumped the block wall in back to an adjacent house. First, I looked up into the trees because a lot of suspects climb up out of sight. When I didn't see anyone, I started crawling around on the ground. My adrenaline was pumping and my heart was racing. I don't think I was frightened; I was just excited. I saw a wooden back porch and I knew there was a crawl space under it. I crept around silently and peered in. There he was, about three inches away from my face. It startled the holy shit out of me. Even though I believed he was under there, when I peeked around under the porch and our noses almost bumped into each other, I lost my strong commanding voice, and instead, using what I thought was my loud command voice, I squeaked out in a very high-pitched tiny little girls voice. "Freeze mother fucker or I'll blow your fucking head off!!" I was so embarrassed. No one else heard me but I heard me, the guy was so scared, that he kept yelling. "Don't shoot me. Don't shoot." The sound of my tiny little voice will be stuck in my head for the rest of my life. I made the arrest but I will never forgive myself. How embarrassing!

Once, we were called to a suspicious circumstances call. A man had called in stating that his ex-girlfriend had planted a large amount of marijuana in his car and he was afraid to drive away because he knew she would call the police and try to get him arrested. When we arrived at the scene, he was waiting patiently there for us and so was his ex-girlfriend. It turned out that he was married and wanted to break off the relationship, but she didn't want to let go. She placed a very large bag of marijuana in the backseat of his car and he was scared to drive away with it there and didn't want to touch it.

In those days, marijuana was very illegal. Well, right away I wanted to arrest her but I couldn't, because we couldn't place the marijuana in her hands. It was her word against his. We ended up doing the next best thing we could do and called our sergeant over. After we explained the conundrum to him, he had a great solution. He examined the package carefully and determined that it wasn't marijuana at all and he didn't want to see us spend the rest of our shift writing this stupid report when we could be out there doing some real police work. He instructed us to dump it down a sewer drain and drive away. He was so cool. They don't make them like him anymore. For that reason, he shall remain anonymous. But you know who you are Jon. All I know is, some rats or homeless bums must have really enjoyed themselves that night.

Another time at band camp...Oh, wait that was another story.

But I do have some Hollywood stories for you. Like the time on one occasion, Gary and I stopped well know big screen actor Donald Sutherland. He was sporting a scraggly beard and mustache as he walked down a residential street. We didn't recognize him at first and thought he was a transient. Even after he gave us his identification, it took us a little while to figure out who he was.

Six months later, we arrested a well-known comedian for swinging an ax at a Maître D in an upscale restaurant. The reason for this outburst was due to the fact that he couldn't get seated as promptly as he expected. He shall remain anonymous.

Gary and I made quite a name for ourselves. We were known as the indestructible duo. No matter what shit we got into, it just seemed to slip right off of us…the Teflon team.

I'll never forget the first time I received an "excessive force" complaint. Come on, five feet two and one hundred and ten pounds? We had arrested one of Liberace's relatives for drunk driving and he decided that he wanted to fight with me. He really wasn't very big, so I was able to take him down easily. Later, I found out that he had filed an excessive force complaint against me. All of the deputies at the station were slapping me on the back and congratulating me. It was my night of glory.

Report writing was very important. The deputies needed to document everything they did for the night. Any incidents or arrests had to have a report documenting everything that happened. One night, Gary and I were patrolling a parking structure. We drove to the top of the structure and got out of the car to check everything out. Neither one of us remembered to close our doors. It was a cold and rainy night. Suddenly, a big mangy, wet dog jumped into the front seat and tore up all of my reports. That was one of the nights that I didn't get home for several hours after my shift was over. I had to rewrite every single report I had written by memory.

The station was across the street from a public park. Many nights after work, the deputies would gather at the park, drink a few beers and unwind. One of the guys was a small built guy and when the guys would get drunk, they would pants this poor son of a bitch and hang him upside down on the flagpole. He was the best sport. He never stopped coming and he had the best arrest record of anyone. He later transferred to the Narcotics Bureau and was credited with some of the most outstanding arrests.

Does anyone remember the first pornographic movie ever shown in a public theatre? It was "Deep Throat" and it opened in West Hollywood and Gary would take me there many times under the guise of looking for perverts. I always hid behind the curtain in the back, but not Gary. He would strut his stuff all the way down the aisle, shining his flashlight at everyone. Sometimes he could be such an asshole. Because of our many arrests, we spent a lot of time in court. The station had a little room in the basement with a few cots in it for those of us that had to work late and get up early in the morning to go to court. We spent many nights on those cots. One night in particular, the cots were already full when we got there. So, I put a blanket on the floor below another deputy's cot. In the morning when everyone was waking up, this deputy, Mike, reached down and touched my shoulder, shaking it and said, "I'm sorry doll, I didn't mean to push you out of bed during the night." Everyone in the room broke into laughter. That was a great memory. I was lucky. No one ever gave me a bad time about being a woman in a man's world. I was treated great by almost everyone, with a few exceptions which I will discuss later. When it came time for my first evaluation by Gary, he wrote this:

Dear Captain Dennison,

I would like to report that during my many rubbing sessions with deputy Caples, many of my outstanding qualities have rubbed off on her. She is doing a fine job and with my further rubbing I believe she will become an excellent deputy.

Signed,
Gary Huffman

The captain was a great sport and accepted that evaluation and placed it in my jacket.

I know it sounds like Gary and I, never did any real police work, because I am sharing all of these with you. But it's the anecdotes I remember most and will always cherish. It isn't important to me that we made great arrests and I'm sorry if that's what you were expecting. I just want to remember all of the really good times I had there.

After the first year, the program was deemed a success and jobs not only opened up locally but all over the United States for women in patrol. We eventually received our pants uniforms, a few years later.

Our department used a ten-code system. That cut down on our broadcasting time and condensed it so the deputies could say what they needed to say in only a few words.

Here is an example of our ten- code:

>Ten-1 Receiving broadcast poorly,
>Ten-2 Receiving well,
>Ten-4 OK,

Ten-6 Busy,
Ten-7 Out of service,
Ten-8 In service,
Ten-19 Return to the station,
Ten-20 What is your location?
Ten-22 Stop all further action,
Ten-97 Arrived at scene,
Ten-98 Finished with last assignment.

The deputies also had another "code" system,

Code-3 Emergency, use red lights and siren,
Code-4 No further assistance needed,
Code-7 Out of service to eat.
Code - 997 Officer needs help
urgently district cars only,
Code 998 Officer involved in shooting,
Code 999 Officer needs help urgently,
call everyone to respond.

As you can see, that was a lot to memorize, plus our penal codes and remembering what streets we were on at any given time. Talk about multi-tasking. To make it even worse, the deputies developed a One-Code system, just to be used between deputies. These were a lot funnier and used only in a joking manner. Example:

101, You gotta be kidding,
102, Get off my fucking back,
103, Beats the shit out of me,
104, WTF? Over,
105, It's so fucking bad I can't believe it,

106, I hate this fucking place,
107, This place stinks,
108, You're an asshole,
109, Beautiful just fucking beautiful,
110, Up your ass,
111, You're a dumb bastard,
112, Let ME talk to that son-of-a-bitch,
113, Big fucking deal,
114, Get your shit together,
115, You bet your sweet ass,
116, Kiss my ass,
117, If you think I'm shitting you just try me,
118, What are you trying to do, make Lieutenant?
119, You piece of shit,
120, You piss me off,
121, If you say "No Hablo" one more time
I'll ram one of your sugar cubes up your ass,
122, Same to you fella,
125, I think I'm gonna puke,
126, Go stuff a bike up your ass,
135, Screw you and the horse you rode in on,
169, Fuck you just fuck you,
169-1, Let's all get laid,
170, Excuse me sir I think you have mistaken
me for someone who gives a shit.

Gary soon moved on to greener pastures and I started working with other good deputies. On New Year's Eve, I was assigned to work with a very nice deputy on PM shift named Darden Hollis. He was always referred to as "The Cat Man" because he loved cats. At the end of our shift, both of us were asked to work overtime for four more hours, because the graveyard shift was short of manpower. We both agreed to work. The station didn't pair us up on that next shift, because there was a reported rape at a nearby station and they needed a woman to interview her. As it turned out, she was a prostitute that didn't get paid by her John so, she reported him for rape. After interviewing her for about ten minutes, that fact became very clear that she was just trying to get paid. Darden was assigned to work with another really nice deputy named Mike. While I was at the other station interviewing the prostitute, Darden and Mike got a call to a sex shop by the security guard advising them that the guy was armed with a screwdriver and had broken the front window.

Darden and Mike arrived at the scene and Mike tried to unarm the guy. In the meantime, two other deputies pulled up in their patrol car to assist. Somehow, the suspect was able to unarm one of the deputies and killed Darden and seriously wounded the other two deputies. Mike was able to get back to the patrol car to call for help and ambulance. Did you notice that in those years we didn't have walkie talkies or body mic's? In emergencies, someone had to run back to the police car and request help over the car radio. Darden died at the scene and one of the deputies was shot in the leg and another was shot in the groin. The deputy that was shot in the groin eventually had to retire with his injuries. As soon as I returned to the station, the Captain requested Mike and me to accompany him to Darden's home to notify his wife of Darden's passing. Our job was to comfort her, in her time of need and keep her mind from focusing on her loss. As soon as she opened the door, I burst into tears. I felt so terrible for her, I just lost all control. She was an English woman and maintained her composure the entire time we were there. She went into the kitchen and came back with snacks and tea for all of us. We stayed with her the entire night, until day shift from the downtown office arrived to relieve us. We wanted to make certain that she was never alone or needed anything. All police and fire departments take very good care of their employees and employee's families. I was fortunate enough to never have to give another death notice to another spouse, the rest of my career. RIP Darden.

They re-assigned me to work with another deputy on my next shift. He used to like to sing the lyrics to old music from the 1940's and 1950's. That was my era too, so many nights while working we would each try to think of a song that the other one didn't know the lyrics to. I know, don't end a sentence with a preposition. But just this once? As much as we tried to stump one another we never did. Both of us knew the lyrics to all of the old songs, so instead we would just sing songs all night together while still making arrests.

RIP Joe.

Whenever we would arrest a female, we would have to transport her to Sybil Brand. I always looked forward to going there and seeing old friends. I was assigned to work the complaint desk for a while. It was a nice change. At that time, we didn't have a 911. Instead, citizens had to call the station directly and we would dispatch the deputies from the station. There was a complaint deputy and a watch deputy. The complaint deputy would take all of the walk-in complaints over the counter and write those reports. The watch deputy would monitor all of our radio cars and dispatch calls to available units.

I kept receiving a call from someone saying that there was a fight or screaming going on in a particular apartment. When our deputies would arrive, everything would appear to be normal. Finally, one night the two gay guys that lived in that apartment showed up at the front desk to complain about all of the harassment these false calls were causing them. They had a young man with them that turned out to be one of their nephews. As soon as I spoke with the young man, I recognized his voice as the one who was making all of the complaint calls.

I went into my lieutenant's office and told him about it. I didn't want to make an arrest over the counter without his prior approval. He went out with me and we told the two men that their nephew was the one making the crank calls. We then asked them if they wanted him arrested. Of course, they were shocked and didn't want to prosecute him, but did say that they would be returning him to his mother at once. Believe it or not, I received a commendation for that. Thank you, lieutenant.

As with any environment there were the bad ones. We had a watch sergeant named Dale Hollingsworth who was a chauvinist pig. He resented me for being one of the first women in patrol, and he also hated me because I refused to "cow-tow" to him. He thought he was a military drill sergeant and would sit in his office - ten feet away - and yell.

"KAYPULLS!! GET IN HERE!!!"

I would completely ignore him. He would yell over and over again and I would never respond. Finally, he would come out of his office and yell, "Kaypulls, didn't you hear me calling you?"

"Oh, no sergeant I didn't. Did you want something?"

I couldn't have been sweeter. He hated me. He knew damn well that I heard him and just refused to acknowledge him. But he couldn't prove it. Ha, ha, ha, Dale, kiss my ass. Another time, while I was watch deputy and assigned to work dispatch, a recruit from the academy came to the station as part of his academy training. Sgt. Hollingsworth changed the assignment roster and made "me", the complaint deputy and the recruit watch deputy in charge of dispatch. He was just trying to disrespect me.

But no way. He was risking the lives of our field deputies putting this recruit in a position like that, especially one that he couldn't handle. I stormed into his office and told him that if he didn't change the assignment roster that very minute, I was going to call the sheriff at home, tell him what he had done, and have his ass reamed. That son of a bitch knew I would get the sheriff out of bed to ream his ass so he changed it. Years later, after I had retired with a disability retirement, he wrote my final evaluation. First, he wrote some good shit about me and then he hit me with the zinger. He wrote, Deputy Kaypulls does not get along well with her fellow deputies and supervisors.

When I received it, I called him on the phone. I explained to him that any negative information was to be written in the sergeant's little black book and it then had to be brought to the attention of the deputy. I told him that none of this was ever written in the little black book, and that it was never brought to my attention. On early morning shift, while the watch sergeant was sleeping, the other deputies and I would sneak in there and read everything in the little black book. Then, I informed the big blowhard that because of that, he was required to remove all negative comments from my evaluation and leave in only the good ones. Then, I hung the phone up on him and called his lieutenant. I explained the situation to him and he assured me that all of the negative comments would be removed and a new improved evaluation would be in the mail the next day. Don't fuck with Kaypulls, Hollingsworth! You are out of your league.

I worked with a great deputy at the desk. He had a good sense of humor and we had some good laughs. He was always amazed at how disrespectful I was to Dale and got away with it. I often reminisce about fucking over him. A smile comes to my face every time.

Another new program opened up and I applied for it and yes you guessed it, got it. It was called job rotation. I was sent to three different divisions to work and one of them was Sybil Brand, but at Sybil Brand I went back as a sergeant.

My first rotation was to the child abuse unit. Everyone in there was certain that the parents were always wrong. I was prepared for the worst. I imagined little bodies broken and damaged. Happily, I never had to see that. Instead, we had a steady stream of little punk brats trying to get their parents arrested for just trying to discipline them. I praise these parents. Raising kids in today's society is very difficult because every little brat threatens their parents that they will have them arrested for child abuse. I say "No!" Parents, stand your ground. Make that little brat grow up right, in spite of himself.

My next assignment was back at Sybil Brand as a sergeant. I was happy to be back at my old stomping grounds. I had already worked all of the places at the prison. So, I felt quite at home going there and spending time with the deputies in their assigned stations. I tried to spend as much time with them up on the floor as I could, instead of sitting with the other 'brass" in the brasses station. I gave the new ones as much insight and help with their duties as possible, so they wouldn't feel so lost. Amazingly, some of the same old inmates were there. Not still, but as new arrestees. Jail is the biggest revolving door on the planet.

My last job rotation was to background investigations. I liked that best of all. When applicants had passed their written and physical tests, they needed to have a thorough background investigation done on them. We were even required to go to their elementary school and check those records and talk to those teachers. We went to every job they had ever had, talked to former employers and fellow employees. This was a lot of leg work. Not to mention gas mileage. It is amazing what you find out about people. We also went to their previous residences and even talked to landlords and neighbors.

I suggest that if you know anyone planning on going on any police department, that you have them read this book first. This book will help them avoid a shit load of pitfalls. Now, the best part of this job was, that we called in "on duty" from home. My partner was a late sleeper, so he had us call in at 8:00 AM, roll over and go back to sleep until 9:00 AM and then meet somewhere to start our day. Then, we would go home around 3:00 o'clock and call off duty at 5:00 o'clock.

I always felt guilty about it so, I would go to work alone on my days off and weekends to finish up work that should have been done during the week. That really pissed my husband off because he couldn't figure out why I didn't just stay home. The sheriff's department had been good to me and I just couldn't screw over them. Anyway, my two months there went by way too quickly and I hated to go. Oh well, back to patrol and that ass hat sergeant.

When I got back, it was work, work, work as usual. I had the opportunity to work with a number of different deputies. All did a good or great job but some were assholes to me.

I guess they assumed that my other partners had treated me badly, so they decided to do it so also. Usually, these guys were not there when I originally arrived and came in later after I returned back from job rotation. When I say badly, I don't mean they ever abused me physically. They could be mentally abusive however. They would do things like not talk to me for the entire shift, and when they did, it was to say something mean.

It was protocol when two partners worked together that one would drive and the other would sit in the passenger seat and write all of the reports for that night. Then, the following night you would shift the duties. This was not the case with many of my partners. They would drive every night and leave me to do all of the reports. I am guessing that you have gotten a pretty good grasp of my personality by now so I know you may find it hard to believe that I would put up with that shit. When I look back it is even hard for me to believe but I did. I didn't want to make every night at work a battle. I had a family at home and wanted to spend my time there in peace. Besides, I had accrued a lot of overtime hours and used a lot of them up going on long weekends away. It broke up the tediousness of it all.

I split up my time up, from going out into patrol and working inside at the desk. During part of this time I fell ill and had to work inside because I was suffering from hypoglycemia, low blood sugar, and had to eat small meals every four hours. It was a nice respite. Inside was every bit as busy as outside. The phones never stopped ringing and the calls had to be dispatched. It was a crazy time, but fun. Then again, I thought everything was fun.

Eventually, I went back out on patrol. That's when the real action began. One night, we went in foot pursuit of a suspect. He ran into an apartment building and tried to close the door. He was trying to close it from the inside and we were trying to push it open from the outside. We pushed with all our might until finally, the door-jam broke and the whole damn door caved inside. Naturally, I was first in line, so I went ass over applecart, into the apartment unit and my fellow deputies were in such a hurry to get in there, they just trampled me in every direction. I ended up in the hospital with both back and neck injuries. Shortly thereafter, I was forced to retire because my injuries no longer qualified me to work in law enforcement. Not a very glamorous ending, right? I couldn't even claim I had been shot. No, I was trampled by my own comrades.

Life can be quite the son of a bitch sometimes.

CHAPTER NINE

Remember me telling you about my husband taking me out to buy a Mercedes? Well, this is the $3.500 car I insisted on buying instead. This little orange car actually saved my life once.

In late November of 1977, I had a run in that I will never forget. This was after I had retired from the Los Angeles County Sheriff's Department and you would think that my life was on cruise control. I was on my way home as I drove over the mountain from a movie in Beverly Hills, on my way to the San Fernando Valley. I always took this same route to and from West Hollywood Station, where I worked. It was lonely windy road. There weren't any street lights or businesses along there, just very exclusive homes.

I was in my little 1972 Z600 Honda car then. It only had 2 cylinders and was a 4-speed stick transmission, but I loved it. It was about midnight and because of the chill in the air, my windows were up. I always drive with my doors locked for security reasons. I also periodically check my rear and side-view mirrors out of habit. During this routine habit I saw an older station wagon coming up the hill behind me at a pretty fast pace. I assumed that he would pass me, but instead, they pulled around me and forced me to the side of the road. There were two male occupants in the car.

Both of them jumped out and ran to my car. When I saw that, I knew I was in trouble. Fortunately for me, my little Honda was a four-speed stick transmission and I was able to throw it into reverse and back out of there. When I had sufficient distance between us, I whipped a U-turn and headed back down the mountain. Well, obviously they had something else in mind. They jumped back in their car, turned it around and sped after me down the mountain. When they caught up with me, they again pulled in front of me forcing me to the side of the road. This time, only the passenger jumped out. Before he could even get to my car, I through it back into reverse, only now I was driving up hill. With only two cylinders I couldn't go very fast up hill in reverse, but I had it floored. The driving skills I learned when the department sent me to a special patrol driving school kicked in and so did my little Honda. It didn't have any power, but because of its tiny size, I could maneuver it on a dime. It had such a good turning radius that I could make a 360 degree turn in it even in a parking space.

It was only too apparent to me what they had in mind, once they were able to catch me. All I could think was, I'm not having any of this shit you assholes! You are fucking with the wrong woman. I had a loaded gun lying on my lap, but I didn't want them to know it. I wanted to look as helpless as possible. I wanted that to be my little surprise, just in case they were able to catch me.

What if they also had guns? The LAST thing I wanted was to expose my gun and end up in a gunfight with them out on that deserted mountain road. Remember, no one had a cell phone at that time so I couldn't call for help. I just had to make the most with the fucked-up hand that I had been dealt. That mountain road was completely black and the exclusive homes were inaccessible from the road. Even if I was able to get into the driveway of one, I could honk my horn and yell "HELP" for an hour and no one would respond. I wasn't about to get myself into that predicament.

We played, cut me off, throw it in reverse, U-turn, cut me off, throw it in reverse, U-turn, all the way over the mountain. All I wanted to do was get to the other side of the mountain, because I knew that LAPD patrols Van Nuys Blvd. This was usually only a thirty-minute drive over the mountain, but because of all of the evasive driving, this trip took almost three hours. When I finally reached Van Nuys Blvd, they were still right behind me. Suddenly, I saw them,

An LAPD car was driving right at me. I whipped another one of my famous U-turns, right in front of LAPD. I knew they would go in pursuit of me for blatantly making that maneuver, but when I did, the station wagon stopped following me, and kept driving assuming that LAPD would stop me and they could get away. Boy, were they in for a surprise.

While LAPD went in pursuit of me, I went in pursuit of the two guys in the station wagon. They immediately turned off of Van Nuys Blvd. and drove into a residential area. I was right on their tail, and LAPD was on mine, with their red lights and sirens blaring. No matter how hard the station wagon tried to evade me, I stayed right on their tail. All of a sudden, I lost sight of the station wagon. Remembering my patrol pursuit driving tactics, as soon as I lost sight of them, I made the first right turn I came to. There they were, like sitting ducks. They had turned into a dead-end street. They were parked at the end of the street, and I stopped at the entry, preventing them from leaving.

Within seconds, LAPD was all over me, like white on rice. LAPD jumped out of their car and immediately started chewing my ass for the illegal U-turn. I tried to explain to them what had happened, but they wouldn't listen to me. All they heard was that the station wagon cut me off and that did not give me the right to pursue them like I did.

One of the LAPD officers was obviously a training officer and the other one was being trained. The one being trained showed an interest in what I was trying to explain to the training officer and it seemed to me that he wanted to pursue it further. On the other hand, the training officer was not interested in anything I had to say. I showed them my Sheriff's credentials, but that just seemed to make the training officer angrier. LAPD didn't have any women in their department and were very prejudiced against them. I asked the training officer if he would at least get identification from the guys in the station wagon, and look in their car for any kidnapping equipment. (like rope, zip ties, duct tape, etc.) but he refused. Instead he told the guys in the station wagon to leave and that he would detain me long enough so that I couldn't follow them anymore. When I finally got home and told my husband what happened, he was furious. He drove me down to the Van Nuys police station and made a complaint to the Watch Commander. The Watch Commander called the two policemen into his office and just told them that they should have followed up on this incident, and then sent us home.

Several years later, I saw on TV that they had arrested two guys in Washington State for murder. It turned out that they were the Hillside Stranglers and had kidnapped, tortured, raped and murdered at least thirteen women in the San Fernando Valley and then left their nude mangled bodies in the hills. As soon as I saw their photos, I recognized them as the two guys in the station wagon that had chased me over the mountain.

KENNETH BIANCHI
SERIAL KILLER

ANGELO BUONO
SERIAL KILLER

LAPD Trainee if you are reading this look me up. I will remember you, and together we will find your old training officer and tell him what a useless piece of shit he is. He prevented you from making the biggest arrest of your career, and may have failed to prevent additional murders of women.

CHAPTER TEN

Eventually my womanizing husband and I moved to a small town in Colorado. I read in the local newspaper that the town was looking to hire a new police chief so I encouraged my husband to apply, and he did.

There were a lot of applicants for the job, including men with a higher rank than my husband. He had retired as a sergeant but gave an excellent interview and got the job. Soon, we moved there full time. I really loved it down there. Lying out in the sun all day and spending my time on our boat floating down the river was our small piece of heaven.

My husband wanted me to open a business to keep me awake the major portion of the day. He was tired of coming home from work at night and hearing me say, "Oh, is it time to wake up already?" So, I opened a gag gift store and a tanning salon.

You may be asking yourself. Why would anyone open a tanning salon in the middle of the Colorado desert? Or for that matter, a gag gift store surrounded by a Native American Indian reservation? Well, it sure beats the shit out of me. In this small town of about 5000 people I decided what they really needed was a high-quality rubber chicken. Needless to say, I was the only store, in town that had one. Fake poop was a big item there and of course, I was well stocked. Some of my other inventory items were: musical underwear, men's and women's edible underwear (four flavors), itching powder, tons of phony food items, shocking pens and lighters, wind up penises that hop all around, neon shoelaces (not as big an item as I had hoped) whoopee cushions of course, and what gag gift store would be complete without the ever-popular fake puke? I can almost feel my pillow and electric blanket now.

About once a week, my husband threatened to quit his job as Chief and retire again. He was too active a person to ever retire. He still got up every morning and went to the gym to work out, and after that, he would drive over to the airport and fly his plane around for another hour or so before heading into work. At least, that was his explanation of where he was at that time of the morning. By now, I really didn't give a damn where he was.

I was just grateful that he left the house at 5:00 AM. I don't even want to imagine the hell it would be for me if he didn't. What would he do at that time of the morning otherwise? You got it. He would wake me the hell up. And there is no telling what he would want. My God, he might even want me to get up and fix him breakfast. I can't talk about this anymore… It's getting too depressing.

So, where was I? Yeah, so when we first moved there, I weighed 115 pounds. Then I jumped up to 133 pounds. That was it. I started going to a fat doctor, not a fat doctor, but a fat doctor in Palm Springs, California. Anyway, to make a long story short, as it turns out, there was a Bob's Big Boy Restaurant next door to the doctor's office. So, six months later, I was a whopping 139 ½ pounds. I just couldn't bring myself to say 140 pounds. You will not believe the diets I tried that year. You have no idea all of the work I put in on diets. I am convinced that there is one food that you can eat and as long as you don't eat any other food, you will lose weight.

That is where "I" came in. I dedicated that entire year testing certain foods looking for just the right one. Hagen Daze Chocolate, Chocolate Chip was the first one I eliminated. I was really quite disappointed about that one. Right after that, Dryers Pralines and Cream also failed. I had really hoped that one would work. But I guess all "scientists" encounter these disappointments. I refused to be discouraged. I eliminated Oreo cookies, Soft Batch cookies, Chocolate Chip cookies, and Hot Cinnamon Scotties Danish Rolls in fast order. Then, my mother inadvertently, gave me another idea. She said that sometimes when she gets hungry, she takes a spoonful of peanut butter and eats it right out of the jar.

Did you know that with just a little bit of dexterity and skill, you can get an entire eight ounces of peanut butter, on one teaspoon? Six down, nine-hundred and forty to go. I tried eating nothing but sweet pickles for three days, but my mouth rebelled and gave me canker sores. Red raspberry preserves are available in a squeeze bottle now. It takes all of the work and mess out of jelly sandwiches. I tried Red Raspberry Preserves with crackers for a while, but I think the crackers may have been a problem.

The first year we were there, I broke my ass. I was using Sam's ass of course, putting up Christmas decorations all over every available inch of our house. I am not exaggerating, for a change. We had a Christmas light on everything. Not to mention Manger Scenes, Moving Santa Clauses and Reindeer and the list goes on and on. Anyway, I was impressed.

The Chamber of Commerce awarded us 2nd place in the competition home decoration category. Really 2nd place? I was pissed. I wouldn't have minded so much, but I SAW first place in my slightly biased opinion. No way. They wrapped a red ribbon across the first-place winner's garage door. Well, the next year, I didn't put a single light outside and our Christmas tree was placed inside the hall closet, where I viewed it privately. I hope you don't get the wrong impression and think I am a poor sport.

In September, of that first year, I was pulled into another local event. The Chamber of Commerce held a 1950's sock hop. It was a huge success and a lot of fun. But, once you have dressed up in your poodle skirt and saddle shoes in an effort to recapture your youth, and fail miserably, it isn't anything you want to do again. So, the following year, just for the hell of it, a few other girls and I got together and decided to whip up an act. We went out and bought bright material and gaudy trim and made matching dresses for our act. They all wore the same color, but, because I was the star, I had my own color. I ordered some short black wigs from my wig supplier then we got a Dianna Ross recording of "Stop in the Name of Love" and worked up a dance routine. I was Dianna Ross, of course. No one in town knew about this so on the night of the dance, we got all dressed up in our Supremes Outfits and waited backstage. The MC gave us this big introduction, about how the Chamber had spared no expense to bring in this famous singing group for their entertainment. The lights went out and when the record started, the spotlight hit Dianna Ross in her bright orange dress with gold sequins up the sides, and her backup singers in their purple dresses and silver sequins. Dianna was holding a humongous dildo with a flashlight inside as a microphone.

As my back-up singers were screwing up their dance on stage, Dianna was moving through the crowd, sitting on all the men's laps and messing up their hair. God! I've missed the spotlight! For the following year, I talked the chamber out of yet another 1950's sock hop and convinced them that we had enough talent to hold a comedy talent show. I Co-MC'ed that event. I am sure that there are a few people like me that don't mind getting in front of a crowd and making a fool out of themselves, Most I am sure like to sit on the sidelines and watch.

In November of every year, the Chamber puts on a Cadillac Dinner. The tickets go on sale in January and are always sold out in one day. Only one hundred and twenty-five tickets are sold for two hundred and fifty dollars each and one ticket admits two people to the dinner.

The money for the dinner is then placed in an interest-bearing account until November. In November, a new Cadillac is purchased to be awarded to the winner. The one hundred and twenty-five tickets - with the purchaser's name on it - are placed in a barrel and drawn out one at a time. As each person's name is drawn, their name goes up on a big board, and they are eliminated. Every so many draws, one hundred dollars, fifty dollars, wine or champagne is given as a consolation prize. The last name pulled, of course, wins the new Cadillac. But it doesn't stop there. A number of "side pools" are started for various amounts of money. They range in price from fifty dollars to five hundred dollars.

The name drawn last in the Cadillac drawing in that pool, wins all of the money in that particular pool. Conceivably, even if your name isn't drawn last in the Cadillac drawing, you could win thousands of dollars, in the "side pools." The first year we were there, after one hundred and twenty-two names were called, our name hadn't been called yet. They asked the three of us to go up onstage. Sam is a wallflower, so he sent me up there. I forgot to mention that when they get down to the last ten or fifteen names that have been called, there are a lot of people trying to buy your ticket. Big money changes hands at this time.

Anyway, we had already decided not to sell our tickets, for two reasons. One, usually the person that needs the Cadillac the least usually wins, and Sam had just bought me a new Cadillac for my birthday. The other reason was, our ticket number was 007 and with Sam being the Chief of Police, and me a retired policewoman, we thought it was a sign. Well, that just shows you what we know! Our name was the next one called, and some guy in the audience bought the last two tickets for ten thousand dollars each. Not all was lost however; we had entered several pools and left there with five thousand dollars in our pockets. It was not a bad night at all.

CHAPTER ELEVEN

The house became a constant work in progress and we are remodeling again. We were adding two more bathrooms and bigger closets. The house was all torn up. The last time we remodeled, I almost ended up in a mental hospital. This time, we have taken precautions. Sam has removed all sharp objects from the house. Yes, I am still accident prone but I will be ok now, this book is being typed so I don't have any sharp pens or pencils lying around.

Poor Sam, he is so conservative and quiet. He would never deliberately draw attention to himself, and I lay awake at nights, trying to think of ways to draw attention to myself. Unfortunately, when I do, he is inadvertently thrust into the limelight right along with me. He wants to die of embarrassment every time.

Something the attention was business related. I had a couple of commercials running on the radio there in town to advertise my tanning bed business. I didn't mention it to him because I knew if he heard them, he would want to leave town.

Here, is one of them.

"Do you know me? You may remember me as the overweight, overdressed, over the hill redhead, with mayonnaise colored white skin, covered with freckles and cellulite. Well, not anymore! I have been going to "Love It Tan." And, in just a few minutes a week, in peaceful, soothing privacy, I have been completely transformed. NOW, I'm an overweight, overdressed, over the hill redhead with a beautiful tan... Covered with freckles and cellulite."

Fortunately, my husband didn't find out about it until it had already been on the air. In face it was already on air for several days. Unfortunately, the way he did hear about it was from total strangers. They were stopping him on the street to tell him how funny his wife's commercial was. Although the question was looming in his head, he was afraid to ask the question floating in it. What commercial? I think he was afraid that they would tell him. I wish that I could say that the commercial brought in a bunch of new business, but it didn't. Instead, my phone was ringing off the hook from people calling to see if I wanted to buy their cellulite removing cream.

Did I mention that our cat of nineteen years had died back then? Well, we certainly didn't intend to get another one, and we haven't...not exactly. A few months after that, at about midnight, there was a baby kitten outside our back door, just crying its eyes out. I brought her in out of the cold, approximately 87 degrees and fed her fancy albacore packed in spring water at $1.87 a can. I stayed up until about 3:00 AM making certain that she was comfortable and not afraid of the dogs. The next morning, Sam went around the neighborhood looking to see if anyone had lost the kitten. He found a ten-year old little girl that claimed it, but she explained that her family was allergic to cats and that it wasn't allowed in the house. To make a long story short, the kitten came over to our house every night to come in and sleep. That smart little kitten figured out how to get into our courtyard, through our open gate, and even how to get in the doggie door, after I tied it open. And, is it my fault that I would prepare myself some fancy albacore to eat, and then place it on the floor, for just a minute while I changed the channel on the television set, only to discover when I returned, that silly little kitten had eaten all of it?

I kept apologizing to that little ten-year old girl when she would come over every day, looking for her kitten. I would explain to her that I had no control over that darned little kitten and that little bugger would come over to our house every night to play with the dogs, and then stay until the next day when she came over to get it. Then, I would throw my hands up in the air in exasperation. Eventually, she bought it. Even though this little black and white kitten, named Oreo, doesn't belong to us, she comes over every night after nine PM, climbs in the doggie door, eats the albacore I prepared for myself, but left it lying around, and then climbs in bed with us and goes sound asleep.

She absolutely loved our dogs and chased them all around the house. She hides behind or under things and then jumps out, bites them in the ass and then runs likes hell. The best part of the whole deal is, last week her parents took the kitten to the veterinarian to get it fixed and they paid the bill. We get the cat and they get the bill. Only in America.

NEWS FLASH, NEWS FLASH, NEWS FLASH . . .
THE RUBBER CHICKEN JUST SOLD!

Sam thought that I was doing so well with my little gag gift store and tanning salon, that he bought me a liquor store/market and car wash to run. Shit, just when I wanted to sit down. That was not one of our better investments. First of all, I am the next to last person that should ever work with the general public. Sam is the last person. My employees were instructed that if they ever saw me anywhere near a customer, they were to throw a net over me and drag me out of there. Face to face sales and customer service is not my bailiwick. Instead of saying, "Good morning may I help you?" I would say, "What the hell do YOU want?"

So much for customer relations.

I am far too outspoken to be anywhere near people, especially if I am expected to be nice to them.

Our store was a few miles away from an American Indian Reservation, and as you may have expected, they were frequent customers. Everything started off pretty well and we were smart enough to hire workers to run the counter instead of placing ME there. One evening, the night clerk called in sick and I was forced to take her place behind the counter. Much to my relief nothing out of the norm happened until at about 1 AM, an American Indian man came into the store and handed me a check for $100. There were no words, and he just handed it to me as if the check spoke for itself. I just looked at it, as though I had never seen one before.

"Ok what can I do for you?" I said.

"Cash it!" he snapped.

Clearly, I figured out that he was not making a purchase; he only wanted me to give him cash for his check.

"Well I don't know you so I can't just cash your check."

"What in the hell are you talking about?" he yelled. "Just cash the God damn check!"

Did I mention that I don't do well with the general public? You can just imagine that it does not get any better when the public has a shitty attitude.

"Again," I said. "You are not a customer of the store and therefore I am not cashing your check."

"If you don't cash my damn check, I promise you that I will start an "Indian Movement" against your store."

My eyes narrowed and I could feel the hair rise on my back.

"I wouldn't give a damn if you started a **_bowel movement_** in my store! Get the hell out!"

Sure enough, the next day, the Tribal Council held a meeting and instructed the Tribe to boycott my store. Within a week, my inventory no longer dwindled and my "sales" improved.

About a week later, an older American Indian pulled up to the front door in some old car and yelled inside of my store. "Your husband is a dead man!"

I walked out to his car and started writing down his license number and description of him. I also wrote a description of his car.

"If you write down my license number," he screamed. "I will kill you too."

"Well," I said. "You will have to wait until I'm finished writing, because if you are planning on killing my husband and I, I'm damn sure going to have your information in writing!!!"

CHAPTER TWELVE

March 31st, 1981, 9:00 PM

One night, Sam decided that he wanted to stop by the store. We parked out in back and walked around to the front. As we approached, we saw that there was a car parked right at the front door, with the engine running and the driver's door open. We looked through the store's window and saw a young man in his early twenties with a 45- caliber automatic handgun behind his back, approaching our cashier. Oh shit! Neither one of us had a gun on us, so Sam ran around to the back-parking lot, to retrieve his gun out of the car. I stayed, watching through the window.

By this time, the young man reached our cashier. They exchanged a few words and then he brought the gun around and pointed it at her head. My heart sank into the pit of my stomach as I watched in helpless horror, mentally preparing to witness my employee get her head blown off. I have never felt so powerless in my entire life.

Then, without warning, it happened! He pulls the trigger to release a shot directly into her face. It was a shot of water from his water pistol. At that same moment,

Sam rounded the corner at full speed, gun in hand and ran directly into the store, pointing his gun at the young man's head.

"Drop the gun or I will kill you where you stand," he ordered.

This stupid kid thought it was a joke and that Sam was also carrying a water pistol. He just stood there and laughed. At this point I'm now running into the store, yelling at the top of my voice.

"Sam, don't shoot him! It's only a toy gun."

I don't think Sam heard one word I said, because his adrenaline was pumping so hard. Even if he did hear me, would he trust what I said? How could I know for sure? I noticed a slight hesitation in his eyes. Does Sam believe me, or do I really know for certain that it is a toy?

"Drop the gun asshole," Sam shouts. "Before I blow your fucking head off."

This is a policeman's nightmare. There stood that dumbass, with the toy gun just smiling. Then I realized something else. It was April Fool's Day morning.

"Sam, stop! It's April Fools," I said.

I don't know for certain that Sam heard me, or whether he wasn't certain that I knew what I was talking about, but he didn't lower his gun. I continued yelling at him, "Sam! It is a toy gun!" I could see a flicker in his movements. He heard me, but he was afraid to believe it, just in case I was wrong.

Finally, the dumb shit got it. (The young man that is, not Sam.) The kid dropped his toy gun. That was way too close. Just what Sam needed, to kill an unarmed juvenile in our store. After both Sam and I stopped yelling at the kid about how stupid he was, I think it finally sunk in just how close he came to dying. If there is anyone out there reading this, take away a serious lesson from this. These types of pranks are not funny, they are stupid. Don't point toy guns at people as a joke. There might just be an off-duty policeman standing there and he won't have any idea that you are only playing. It is a good way to get yourself killed and the policeman will never get over it. This is no laughing matter.

The next day, our little dog Wonton died unexpectedly. This was definitely one of the shitiest April Fool's Day ever. We had Won Ton cremated and his urn is in my living room today.

That May I was doing as much as possible to get my mind away from the previous month. I went to a Soroptimist, "Ladies Night" and won a paddle boat cruise down the Mississippi River and then on to the Kentucky Derby for a week. We didn't want to go, so we sold it. Then, I bought a VFW raffle ticket and won a Mexican cruise. We didn't want to go to that either, so I gave it to my mother and my aunt for Christmas.

In July, I had to have my little dog Nusher put to sleep. She was old and in a lot of discomfort and I couldn't bear to see her suffer. When I get old and sickly, I hope someone loves me enough to have me put to sleep. But I don't think we have progressed to that point yet. I had Nusher "Freeze-dried" in a sleeping position. Now both she and Wonton can sleep in my living room. Side by side. I had to put Nusher in a glass case, because my new cat Weasel thinks she is beef jerky. That worked out so well, that I have decided to have Sam freeze dried, providing he dies first of course. But in Sam's case, I'm going to have him lying on his back with his knees bent, his arms raised with a hard on. That way, he can double as a coffee table... and other handy things.

In October, 1981, I volunteered to put on a Halloween comedy show as a fundraiser for the Chamber of Commerce. I dressed up as Elmira, Elvira's much older and much fatter sister. I was the mistress of ceremonies. What a BUST! No pun intended. In November, we again went to the Cadillac Dinner. We didn't win the Cadillac, (fooled you) but we did walk away with about $7.000 dollars. Before you get to thinking that we are the luckiest people in the world, you don't have to wonder, we probably are.

Before I can tell you about 1982, I have to digress a little bit. The first year Sam was Chief of Police was in 1981; one of his policemen shot and killed one of the Native Americans from the reservation. Since a Native American was killed, it had to be investigated by the FBI, the BIA, the State, the County and the City. All concurred, it was a justifiable shooting, and clearly in self-defense. Did I say ALL concurred? I meant all except the Native American community. As far as they were concerned, self-defense is not a good enough reason. They demanded that Sam be fired for training his policemen to kill Native Americans. They sent letters to the Mayor, the newspaper, and anyone else they could think of. It finally died down and for the most part, went away. It was a very sad time for everyone.

Then in May of 1981, yet another Native American was shot and killed by one of Sam's policemen. Another sad time for all. Again, unavoidable and self-defense was the finding of the FBI, the BIA, the State, the County, and the City but not the Native Americans. This time it didn't go away. They called the Governor and the Justice Department.

In September, of that same year, there was another police shooting involving a Native American. Now, the shit really hits the fan. We were getting death threats and so were our employees. (We both felt very badly for the families of the slain Native Americans, as well as for the policemen that had to do the shootings. These things have a way of affecting a lot of people). Our employees were followed home and told that if they came back to work for us, they were going to die. Needless to say, we couldn't have them come back to work.

The Native American community finally was able to get an unbiased observer from the Justice Department to come down and hear their grievances. Did I say unbiased? When she arrived in town, she interviewed the Mayor and the Town Council for about twenty minutes. Then, she interviewed Sam for about ten minutes. After that, she went down on the reservation and spent about a month down on the reservation. Sure, sounds like an unbiased observer to me. Did I mention that she was also Native American?

One day, about a month later, she pulled into the parking lot of my store and got out of her car to come in. I have no idea for what reason. Just at that moment, there was a minor fender bender at the intersection at the corner of my store.

One little old lady plowed into another little old lady and one of them panicked, stepped on the gas, jumped the curb and ran right up over you know who. I heard the crash and ran outside. I didn't even know who it was because I had never seen her before. I called for an ambulance and tried to put paper under her because the pavement was hot. The ambulance arrived and took her to the hospital.

Later, a doctor from the hospital called Sam and told him who it was and that she refused treatment until she could call the Justice Department. When she got them on the phone, she informed them that the Chief of Police had tried to have her murdered. Within hours, the place was swarming with Federal Agents. They immediately interviewed Sam and the two little old ladies. The implication was that Sam and the two little old ladies had conspired to kill her.

These poor little ladies were scared to death. I laugh about it now but it wasn't funny at the time. At least in a bad dream, you eventually wake up. No such luck here. As far as I know, the FBI are still investigating her accusations.

The families of the three deceased Native Americans filed a three-million-dollar lawsuit against Sam. The claim was that he had violated the deceases' civil rights. It doesn't matter that we were at home in bed during all three of the shootings; the buck has to stop somewhere. They were unable to prove their case, and it was dropped. Usually, I like to add a little humor to my stories, but some of this stuff just isn't funny.

On January fifth, I stayed home from work sick. At about 2:00 PM. the doorbell rang. Now mind you, I wasn't supposed to be at home. When I opened the door, who do you think was there? It was none other than the same Native American that threatened to start an Indian Movement against us. He was as shocked to see me, as I was to see him. He was there with another guy, and when I opened the door, they fell all over themselves trying to think of a reason they were there.

Usually, neither Sam nor I were ever at home, because we both had to work. One of them finally said that they were selling firewood door to door. I didn't believe them, so when they left, I followed them. Not only didn't they have any firewood, they didn't stop at any other houses to try to sell any. I found this to be very suspicious, so I phoned Sam at work and told him about it. He left immediately to come home, but when he got into our gated community, he saw their car parked at someone's house, so he stopped there. Sam told them that they were on private property and that if they didn't have legitimate business there, they would have to leave. Words were exchanged and they left.

I'll be a monkey's uncle. The next thing we knew, was, the Sheriff notified us that Sam was under arrest for kidnapping. Sam had parked in such a manner that they were unable to move their car. He was also charged with disorderly conduct. They said Sam used foul language. Anyone that knows us knows that Sam didn't use foul language, that was…well is my specialty. I'm the only one that ever-used foul language. Oh, and he was also charged with assault with a deadly weapon. They claimed that even though Sam never actually pulled a gun or pointed it at them, they knew he carried a gun and Sam had a look in his eyes that made them believe that he wanted to kill them. That part was probably true, but Sam had left his gun at the station and didn't even have one with him.

Before I go any further, I need to digress again. The Sheriff was just like the ones you see in all of the movies that Burt Reynolds starred in. You know, cowboy hat, cowboy boots, 32-inch pants under his 50-inch big beer gut, chewing tobacco and spitting it everywhere. Well, the Sheriff was coming up for election and he was so afraid that Sam was going to run against him, that when he got this complaint, he ran with it. It was so obvious that the Sheriff had coached these guys that it was pathetic. They didn't know anything about what could constitute a kidnapping or what disorderly conduct consisted of, and certainly not assault with a deadly weapon when no firearm or knife was present.

Little did the dumb bastard know was that Sam didn't even want to run for Sheriff. He didn't even want to be Chief of Police anymore. Sam was well liked in the community and that worried the Sheriff. Sam was always very tough on crime and especially drug crime. The Sheriff and the County Attorney were not. As a matter of fact, it was next to impossible for Sam to get the County Attorney to prosecute any drug busts. When Sam's policemen made drug arrests, and the County Attorney refused to prosecute them, on several occasions, Sam went directly to the State's Attorney General. A State Police officer told Sam that the Sheriff was under investigation of drug crimes and not to confide in him about any drug matters. When the Sheriff and the County Attorney heard about this complaint, they jumped on it. They couldn't have been more jubilant. Not only, did the Sheriff file the complaint, the County Attorney prosecuted Sam and it went before a Grand Jury. Sam was sent to trial and we had to hire an attorney from a neighboring big city to come and represent him. We were in court for three months.

By that time, Sam and I had enough of small towns and yearned for the lights of the big city. Actually, Sam wanted to leave two years earlier, but since that is what the Native Americans wanted, we decided to stay just to piss them off. It made sense to us at the time. Anyway, we sold our business for pennies on the dollar and on April 1st, Sam resigned as Chief. That date seemed appropriate under the circumstances. On August the first, we packed up our cat and headed for Las Vegas, NV. We purchased a five-bedroom home, just in case we decided to have more children…just kidding.

CHAPTER THIRTEEN

It is just by chance that this ended up being chapter thirteen. I couldn't have planned it any better.

We loved it in Las Vegas. It is so cheap to live here. It is cheaper to go out to eat three meals a day than it is to cook at home. If that sounds a little farfetched, don't say anything to Sam, I have him convinced. Sam joined a gym and said that he went every day. I am waiting until scientists can prove inconclusively that exercise is safe for overweight women in their forties before I commit to anything.

We purchased an apartment building and I ran it for close to ten years. After that, I hired a 25-year-old-girl to manage it. After a few years and near our 40th year anniversary, Sam announced that he and the young girl were moving in together and he was leaving me. He died of cancer in 2006 and left her in charge of the apartment building. Then the housing boom took a dump and she lost the building in foreclosure. I grieved for a few months, until I met a handsome younger man, 28-years my junior. We are going on our 20th year together. He is my best friend. Wish me luck…

EPILOGUE

On June fifteenth 2017, my dear friend and mentor, Geo Owen Fairchild, passed away at the age of 90 years old, with his devoted wife Thelma at his side. Unfortunately, he fell and broke his leg and shoulder. When he realized that his recovery time was going to take a long time, he just sort of gave up and died. He had survived several heart attacks, motorcycle injuries and many other setbacks over the years, but this time, I think he was ready to go.

NOW FOR THE REST OF THE STORIES!

Many other retired West Hollywood deputies have some wonderful stories that they would like to tell. This next group of stories are from them.

CATCH OF THE NIGHT

By Paul Harman (West Hollywood
Deputy 1968-1972)

One cool foggy early morning shift in 1970, Steve Huss and I were working 91 EM's and I was slowly driving the back alleys blacked out with our windows all the way down, listening for any unusual sounds. I looked over and Steve was zonked out, too many work and court days and not enough sleep. No one likes their partner oblivious to what is going on and so I slammed on the brakes, and bailed out of the car and said there he goes! Poor Steve woke up with a start and scrambled out of the car, saying where, where? I said hopefully now you are awake, I don't need you asleep in case we fall into something. Steve was wide-awake after that and we grabbed a cup of coffee just to make sure he stayed that way.

We were hoping to catch a burglar, and went back to patrolling alleys in our patrol area. What we actually caught was much more fun, an LAPD early morning patrol car was backed into an empty sub-garage of an apartment under construction. We tip toed up to their car and both officers were sound asleep. I guess they were catching some sleep out of sight of their patrol sergeant.

Because of the ongoing rivalry between our departments, we decided to place Hold for Sheriff stickers all over their radio cars front windshield. Stifling our laughter, and grinning from ear to ear, we plastered the whole windshield and they never awakened. For good measure, we also put Hold for Sheriff stickers on their back bumper. It must have been interesting when they got a call or woke up and decided to head in for the evening. It must have been a bear to scrape them off too, but who could they tell? It was really tempting to leave the alley Code 3 but we didn't want to awaken the whole neighborhood. I always wondered if they washed off the window but didn't check the back bumper and parked in their station with it that way.

STUDIO ONE

BY Chief Roy Brown, Retired

My older brother (unfortunately recently passed) came to the station to have lunch with me one day. I asked Deputy Lovette Caples if she would escort him to my office when he arrived, but to make him take a search position on the wall outside my office first and then for her to pat him down. She, was ready to go! She made him lean on the wall, legs apart and began to pat him down, based upon a need to conduct a security check before she would allow anyone into the Captains office. I could hear him titter during the pat down and when he entered the office, he busted out laughing. By the way, he commented on how good looking she was.

Next story: Jim Smith was a lieutenant watch commander. I used to come to work for an evening shift every couple of weeks as WHD really had two distinct constituencies. The daytime business/residential community and the nighttime club group and I thought it was important that I connect to both. So, Smith and I, both in soft clothes, (out of uniform) visited Studio One, the large gay night club on Robertson Blvd. We visited with Scott Forbes, the manager, who filled me in on what was going on at the club. As we walked across the dance floor heading to the exit, with about 600 males gyrating to the sounds of the Village People, Jim suddenly stopped, turned and said, '…hey asshole, that's a good way to get busted!' It seems one of the guys groped Jim and he acted reflectively. When he said that I imagined the next day's headline, something about two cops getting their asses kicked trying to make a stupid arrest of a gay man who was among 600 other gay men. I grabbed Jim and suggested we leave…pronto. WHD was a great station, especially before they incorporated, we had a great staff for the most part and my assignment there was one of the highlights of my career.

Roy Brown, LASD Chief, retired

MY TIME

By Commander Lynda Castro

As a patrol deputy assigned to Industry Station in the early 1980's, I worked overtime at West Hollywood Station's Pride Parade. Captain Rachel Burgess inspired me to keep an eye out for a chance to work there.

My dream came true in Aug. 2000, when I was selected as the new captain, replacing Richard Odenthal who retired and went to work as the Public Safety Director for the City of West Hollywood.

There had been contract concerns raised by the community. After a close vote just before I arrived, the contract was renewed and my goal was to ensure safety, security and trust. Community Based Policing, Bike Teams, Foot Beats as well as Segway's at Universal City Walk were innovative and enjoyed by many.

The deputies, thru an MOU, worked 12 hour shifts and were champions at it. Community Based Policing, Bike Teams, Foot Beats as well as Segway's at Universal City Walk were innovative and enjoyed by many. I was promoted in April 2003, passing the baton to Captain Dave Long...West Hollywood was my favorite assignment- there is nothing more fulfilling than being in command of a Sheriff's Station. I retired in 2009 as the Equity Commander after we collectively made great efforts to satisfy the Bouman Consent Decree. The Department was released from oversight by the federal court and it was my time....

WEST HOLLYWOOD STORIES 1973-1976

by Marla Lohneiss (Blomer) Dike

The usual career track for a new deputy back in 1974 was at least two years working in the county jails. But because of the federal push for more females in law enforcement, especially patrol, I actually spent only 10 months at the jails, half at Sybil Brand Institute for Women, and half at Men's Central Jail.

The call went out for transfer requests to patrol, and just like that I was back at West Hollywood Station where I had previously worked as a Reserve Deputy.

Most newly transferred deputies were immediately assigned to a training officer and began patrol training. I, on the other hand, got assigned to the desk, 90D. Luckily, I was somewhat familiar with the area having worked as a Reserve but the desk maps certainly didn't show me where all the alley shortcuts were. I did take a lot of reports over the counter and searched many females brought in to the jail. But some were not really females.

One night on PM shift one of the patrol units brought in a tall, well-dressed woman and asked me to pat her down thoroughly before they put her in lock up.

I was working my way down her torso when I discovered some extra equipment in the crotch area. Then I noticed the Adam's apple and knew I'd been had! It seems the boys tried this on every female deputy. But I never made that mistake again!

Finally, I got off the desk and out on patrol with my official training officer, Jim Campbell. We were assigned car 93 Early Mornings (11 PM to 7 AM) on 19 Feb 1976, my very first night in the field. PM crews were working a 245 ADW (attack with a deadly weapon) that turned into a 187 PC (homicide) and we were to assist them. The victim, found lying in an alley with a fatal knife wound, was the actor Sal Mineo. As the trainee I got to beat the bushes around the scene searching for a knife that might be the murder weapon, but I couldn't find it. I still don't know if it was ever recovered or if anyone was ever prosecuted for his murder.

Part of what made working WHD so interesting was its boundaries. It was a county island surrounded on the west by Beverly Hills and all other sides by the City of

Los Angeles. That means LAPD. More than once LAPD officers sent a rape victim to WHD because they knew there was a female deputy on duty. But with just a question or two like "where did this occur?" Oh, that's in the city, not the county. We had to send the victim back to LA city.

There were many situations where being female was a definite advantage. For instance, being a bit smaller, my arm could fit inside a partly open car window and unlock the door when my partner couldn't. Many times, I could sweet talk a drunk into my patrol car for a trip to jail without having to fight him. Diffusing domestic incidents was also a bit easier when the female involved felt I could empathize.

One night we had a call for a 459 (burglary) now in an apartment sub garage off Santa Monica Blvd. Another unit had found one suspect hiding under a car, but a second suspect was still at large. My job was to keep the under-the-car suspect where he was until further back up arrived. So, I kept my gun aimed at him and warned him repeatedly that if he moved, I'd shoot him! He must have believed me because he kept telling the jailor about "that crazy bitch with a gun."

Often my TO (Training Officer) wanted to show me the more colorful spots around the area, such as the Pleasure Chest and the Pussycat Theater. So of course, we had to do thorough patrol checks, especially when "Deep Throat" was showing. Being female and new to this all-male club, I couldn't let any of this bother me. Usually I just rolled my eyes at them and muttered, "really?"

Some interesting people come through West Hollywood. Some claimed to be friends of the Sheriff (FOS), and some really were. Then there were the celebrities. One day I stopped a driver to find out why he had two different license plates on his black and white station wagon. Turned out it was Rudy Vallee and the Connecticut plate were his special reserve officer designator. The California plate was just a regular license.

Another time I stopped Leonard Nemoy, I don't remember what for. It was really a thrill meeting him since I'm a big Star Trek fan. He was playing Sherlock Holmes at Century City then and invited me to attend.

I did go to the play and also got to meet him back stage after the show. Very cool! Another deputy I partnered with was and is a huge Olivia Newton John fan. She had an office on Sunset Blvd, so of course we had to make a stop there for a patrol check.

Then there was the time my partner and I got a call of a man down at one of the nicer apartment buildings off Sunset Blvd. We arrived just after the paramedics and the man was already definitely deceased. The woman who had called, and who lived in the apartment, wasn't giving us much information. Who was he? Where did he live? Did he have any next of kin we could notify? The more we questioned her, the more the situation looked like a business arrangement. In other words, she was a hooker. The only personal item we could find was the man's keys. And his car was a Jaguar. So, I went down to the street and started looking. Jags aren't that common, even in West Hollywood, so eventually I found it about a block away. I opened the door and the glove box. There was his wallet with ID and a phone number. But how was I going to explain to his wife how he died? Having sex with a hooker? I opted to leave notification to the Detective Bureau.

Expect anything in West Hollywood. How about a call of a naked man up a tree in the traffic island on Santa Monica Blvd. opposite the Winchell's Donut House? Or the two guys in the restroom at the park opposite the old station on San Vicente?

Or just guys walking the streets in the neighborhoods off Melrose "waiting for a friend"?

Most of the male deputies I worked with seemed ok with my presence, especially when it came to interviewing rape victims. Of course, they were constantly making sexual references which I and the other female deputies took with good humor, then gave back at them! Lots of innuendos flew across the briefing room, but we all knew that we had to trust each other in the field. One way we bonded was by going out after work for a beer or two. We also played baseball in the park across the street, patrol vs DB (Detective Bureau). Spilling someone's beer on base was an automatic out!

One of my good friends was Irene P. We had been partnering a few times on PM shift, and then worked day shift together. She zipped around in a Mary unit writing parking tickets from a little three wheeled cart and I was a regular patrol unit. One day everyone got a call of a robbery in progress. Irene was closest to the location so she responded Code 3. Imagine a canvas covered three-wheeler careening around corners with red lights and siren! But she got there first! The handling unit took over even though Irene was more than willing to take it and do some real police work – not just writing parking tickets.

On day shift I spent a lot of time writing burglary reports. One of the more well-known victims was Telly Savalas. Some of the reports were just silly. One victim was trying to explain to me exactly what was taken, but he was having a hard time. How can you claim that someone stole your stash of marijuana when possession is illegal? I assured the guy that I would not list it with the other stolen property.

Universal Studios was part of the patrol area and we took advantage of it for training purposes. In the 70's universal was still just a movie studio, not a theme park, and it had some great sets from well-known movies such as Psycho, Jaws, and the house from Ozzie and Harriet. ★ As a Reserve, I played victim and/or witness in various scenarios. Later we used the motel set and the town square for ongoing role playing and training. Very fitting. West Hollywood using Hollywood for police training.

I thoroughly enjoyed my time on patrol at WHD. Working the desk was not as much fun, but it was a challenge keeping track of all the units before the age of computers and GPS. Being a female working the desk was an advantage – multi-tasking was easy for me. I memorized most of the area addresses and every important phone number and could quickly tell callers which agency could help them if we could not. I worked with some great peace officers and to this day I am very proud of having been a Los Angeles County Deputy Sheriff.

CADET ON PATROL

By Bob McCarty

In 1970 I worked WHD on a PM shift as a cadet out of academy Class 141. I ended up as a third man in one of the cars. I think it was 96. During the shift we were assigned to work the boulevard. The two deputies began walking the street and I was told to patrol and listen for our call sign and return to the boulevard to pick them and a prisoner up. I think it was unheard of to let a cadet take over the wheel and patrol the boulevard and the neighborhood. While on the boulevard, a vehicle traveling the same direction in front of me, swerved. in an attempt to hit a deputy that was directing traffic around an accident scene. I activated the lights and siren and the deputy began shouting "go get that xxxxxx". I broadcast the pursuit and several blocks later 90S (90 Sgt.) pulled behind me. The unit turned on a side street and I positioned my unit slightly to the left with 90S still in the right portion of the roadway. Apparently, with the suspect seeing two units behind him he pulled over and we positioned our units for safety and eventually took the suspect into custody. 90S called for another vehicle to transport the suspect to the station. I was directed to return to patrolling the boulevard and shortly the deputies rejoined me and we resumed normal patrol.

The first thing on Monday morning, at inspection I was directed to immediately report to my DI. He said he received a phone call from WHD Station advising him of an incident I was involved in. He wanted me to relate what happened that caused the station brass to call him. Thinking something bad was about to happen, I related all the incidents we were involved in and the arrests we made. At this point he smiled and stated the brass called him to relate the same and gave me an outstanding evaluation.

THE COLORS

By Assist. Sheriff, Duane Preimsberger, retired

The flat roofed, almost windowless, gray, concrete block, utilitarian building on the southwest corner of Compton Ave. and Nadeau St. had been built in the early 1950's and almost fifty years later it had pretty much outlived it's useful life as a Los Angeles County Sheriff's Department Station. Hundreds of Deputy Sheriffs had served portions of their careers while assigned to this facility. A few of them were truly exceptional law enforcement officers, many were average, some bordered on mediocre and a few were rogues who ended up disgracing the badge they wore and these were sometimes fired or prosecuted. Occasionally, there were unusual individuals who fit neatly into none of these categories.

The old, tired Station had existed in an area that had seen tremendous changes in demographics. It had seen white flight in the early fifties, a preponderance of blacks in the sixties and seventies and a huge increase in Hispanics in the eighties, nineties and beyond. Along with the changes in people it had seen changes in activity. Never a well to do area, the Station jurisdiction had been at the focal point of inner-city riots in 1965 and 1992. It became a haven for undocumented immigrants from both Mexico and others from a hodge-podge of South American countries.

Rampant unemployment, drug and alcohol abuse, broken families, gangs, guns and a host of social ills created a big blip in both crime and the level of activity for those who policed the area. It was a very busy and often dangerous place in which to wear a badge.

As the problems in the area grew, the brass in the Sheriff's Department added more and more personnel in an effort to try to keep a lid on street crime. The addition of new people quickly overloaded the Station's ability to house them and literally wore it out. It wasn't long before a decision was made to add more facilities to the area.

The old Station's area shrunk and with it so did the volume of work for its staff. Two additional Sheriff's Stations, one in Carson and a second in Lynwood absorbed much of the work and personnel. Additionally, the Department had committed to build a huge, modern, regional Station that would absorb all the people presently assigned to Firestone and Lynwood: allowing future expansion and growth and permitting the closure of the two older facilities.

Along the way, Firestone Station had somehow become a place from which legends emanate. Since it was in a less desirable neighborhood, it wasn't a place where many people volunteered to go. Turnover was frequent as those who had been drafted to work there transferred to other Stations closer to their homes. Aside from Detectives and Station Sergeants and Lieutenants, anyone with more than 3 years of patrol experience was viewed as an experienced Patrol Deputy and most of these were in their twenties and thirties.

These young, mostly male, Deputy Sheriffs began to identify themselves as a special breed: they saw themselves as individuals who were working in a hostile environment, one that was much different from assignments to the other twenty plus Stations within the Department. They called themselves, "Stoney Boys," and enjoyed the status that went with working at what they believed was the toughest patrol assignment in the Department.

Older, more experienced, former members of the Firestone Station complement listened in quiet amazement as those presently assigned talked of the demands upon them and the dangers they faced. In the three Station area, the evening watch, from 4 PM to midnight might field as many as 50 patrol cars. The grumpy old timers remember the early sixties when 10 cars policed the same areas without SWAT teams, portable radios, helicopters, night vision goggles and dog handlers.

"These new kids don't know what tough is, somebody ought to piss on their leg so they'll at least smell like a real Deputy," muttered one of the grumps. What the grumps failed to consider was the growth in calls for service, the ever-increasing demand for reports of all kinds, more gun violence on the streets, new legal constraints on police activity and the civil liabilities and threats of lawsuits confronting the current batch of patrol Deputies. In either era it was unquestionably a tough place to work.

Al Winston was a 29-yr. old Deputy Sheriff with six years on the job. For the last two plus years he had been at Firestone Station, sent there by the Department. He was assigned to work the Station Desk and counter on the very last shift at the Station.

At around midnight, the last Firestone Station patrol unit would leave the streets, the doors would close, the lights would go out and a page in the history of the Los Angeles County Sheriff's Department would be turned. The phones and operations would be switched to Century Station.

Everyone there that evening was in a somber mood. Although few of them had asked to be assigned there, all felt that they were losing something special with the closure of the Station. Al was monitoring the dispatch area radio at midnight and listening as, one by one, the patrol units returning to the Station went off duty. "Firestone unit eleven- one, one, is 10-7 (out of service) for the last time," an emotion charged voice from the field announced.

"Firestone eleven, one, one, final 10-7, thanks for your service," responded the radio operator.

By one o'clock in the morning most of the members of the last shift at the Station had retired to a nearby park to reminisce and drink some beer. Each Deputy had a favorite story to tell about an experience at the old place. By four o'clock the park was empty except for a couple of beer cans glistening in the dew of a very early morning. The old building sat quiet and dark on its corner for the first time in fifty years. Those who left the park managed to drive by and take one last, heavy-hearted, look at the place.

Al hadn't wanted to work the desk on the last night; he'd rather be on the street in a patrol car. However, his lieutenant had been on his case because of Al's track record for the use of force in making arrests. He didn't think there were. "He likes the troops and they like and respect him," Al thought.

As usual for a well-liked Captain, there was a big retirement party with hundreds of well-wishers. There were a lot of awards and presentations for Odie from the Department and allied organizations. Although Al wasn't on the program, he'd brought something for Odie that he thought the Captain might like to have.

As the evening wore on, Commander Bill Mc Sweeny, the Master of Ceremonies was in the process of bringing the event to a close and that's when Al got to his feet and made his way forward with his present.

"I got one more thing to give him," Al said in a voice that was starting to choke up.

Mc Sweeny called the program back to order and the hundreds of guests retook their seats, wondering what the young man at the microphone and podium was going to do.

Al had a tough time talking, he hadn't intended it to happen, it just did. His voice quavered and broke with emotion as he spoke about Odie, the man who had helped him and probably had saved his career, a guy that the troops loved and respected because they knew he cared about them. Those who were listening were aware that Al was speaking from his heart and that he was trying his best to do something meaningful for the man they honored this night.

"Captain," he said as he opened a large brown paper bag, I took this flag home with me on the night that Firestone Station closed for the last time. I think it's very special. I wanted to give it to you for saving my job and I know you worked at Firestone for a long time and I think that it would be a good thing if you had this. Thanks for all you did for me and everybody else, I want you to have The Colors."

For a moment there was silence from the audience and then, in unison, those assembled came to their feet and wave after wave of applause echoed through the room as Al and Odie stood together.

Odie held the flag case in one arm and the other was around the shoulder of one of his troops. Many of those who watched were thinking to themselves that there could not have been a finer closing or tribute to a career well spent.

The tattered and worn flag, dressed up in the glass and wooden presentation case didn't make the flashy impression that the other awards had made, those from the desk of a politician, agency head or organization. The others were momentos and tokens that couldn't compare or match this Presentation of Colors, a torn and worn flag that meant much to those assembled, the man giving it and the man receiving it. It was one of those once in a lifetime moment forever treasured. It was a gift that had come after thoughtful reflection and it came from the heart.

Odie had teared up a little and he too was having difficulty getting his words out. All he could say as the evening came to a very special close was, "Thanks Al, I'll keep and treasure these Colors forever."

He decided that he'd keep the U.S. flag and give the California one to one of the other desk Deputies. The U.S. flag rode home with him on the front passenger seat later that night. He bought a mahogany and glass presentation case for the flag and kept it on a shelf in his living room. He'd point it out proudly to his friends and family as a treasure from the place in the Los Angeles County Sheriff's Department where "real" Deputies once worked.

Al's assignment to West Hollywood Station has been a pleasant surprise to him. He'd been assigned to a patrol car working a late evening watch starting at 7:00 PM and going until 3:00 AM. The activity level was fairly significant and he enjoyed the new environment more than he thought he would. His fellow Deputies were pretty good people and they had accepted him as somebody who had paid some dues on the street. What was really interesting to him was the affection that they had for the Station Captain, Dick Odenthal.

"He takes care of the Deputies, he's a stand-up guy. If you're right, he's behind you all the way. If you make an honest mistake, he won't kill ya. But if you don't do your job or you're a genuine turkey or screw-up or if you lie to him, he'll hand you your head. Best of all, he's a cop's cop"

It was a week before Al met him and it didn't occur in the Captain's office like he thought it would. Al and his partner were working West Hollywood unit 92A, (Ninety-two Adam) when they were dispatched to meet 90 C

(Ninety Charlie) at Sunset Blvd. and San Vincente Ave. at 10 PM on a Thursday night. It took them about 10 minutes to wind their way through the usual West Hollywood traffic congestion and locate 90C, Captain Odenthal.

"Odie," the nickname by which his troops and practically everyone else in West Hollywood as well as the Sheriff's Department called him, was standing on the south-west corner awaiting their arrival.

He wasn't hard to spot in the midst of stylish, trendy, affluent; area residents and the punk rockers with purple hair and nose and navel rings. Odie was about six feet tall, balding, about 50 pounds overweight and wearing an outfit that looked like it had recently been hanging in a Salvation Army Thrift Shop.

"That's our Captain?" Asked Al. "Looks like a fat Columbo to me."

"Maybe so, but he's spent more time on the street than probably the whole evening shift combined and I wouldn't want to mess with him."

They parked their patrol car in a taxi zone and walked the short distance to their Captain. "Hi, you must be Al Winston, I'm Dick Odenthal. Welcome to West Hollywood Station, I'm glad to have you here."

"Thank you, sir."

"You guys mind taking a walk with me?"

"Al, I don't like to spend all my time riding a desk so I try to get out here in the field with you guys so I can see what's going on in the streets. You may be accustomed to a first meeting with a Captain in an office, but I think most Deputies are not real comfortable there so I'd rather come out and meet here in your office.

The three of them walked along Sunset Blvd. past dozens of people heading for restaurants, nightclubs, stores and markets while Odie did the talking.

"This is a really interesting and unusual place to work, most of our community holds us in pretty high regard and that's good.

We operated this Station and police this city under a contract and that means if we don't do a good job, West Hollywood gets somebody else to do their cop stuff or they can start their own police department. Al, that's pretty important for you to remember. How you do your job here has implications for everybody not just you. If you screw things up a whole bunch of really good people could be transferred to less desirable places. In a way it's much different than working at Firestone Station, there's more riding on individual performance.

I didn't come out here to tell you that you did a bad job someplace else. What's important to me is what kind of job you do here for the people who pay for us- as well as for the other Deputies who depend on you, that's all I'm interested in. I'm sure you've heard enough motivational speeches in your career and I'm not going to do that to you. As a matter of fact, I'm only going to insist that you do two things while you work here and neither is too big of a deal to accomplish.

First, be honest. I want you to be able to look yourself in the eye in the mirror every morning that you work here and to be sure that the guy looking back at you is somebody with personal and professional integrity.

I want you to be honest with the people we serve- even the bad guys, as well as with the Department and the folks that work with you. That star on your chest is a badge of honor, it means a whole lot to me and to a whole lot of others who have worn and are wearing it. Second, I want you to do a good job. I expect the kind of performance from you that you'd be happy for your mom to see on T.V. So, if you do your job as if Channel 7 News was filming you through the entire shift, I won't be disappointed.

If you give me those two things, I'll do what I can to help you assure that working here is something you like doing. I'll help you find another job in the Department if, after a while here, you want to move on. I'll help you try to get promoted if that's what you're interested in and I'll back you up if you're in a tight spot. Any questions, Al?

"No sir, you've made it pretty clear and I appreciate that. Thanks for coming out and doing this in the field, you're right it's a better way to meet than across a desk."

After covering about four blocks, the trio reversed their path and returned to the starting point. The conversation drifted to topics about where Al went to school, where he lived, what he did in his off time and questions about family. Again, at the corner of Sunset and San Vincente, they shook hands. Odie left them and they returned to the patrol car in the taxi zone.

"That was unusual," commented Al.

"He's not your usual guy."

The first days at West Hollywood Station turned into weeks and months. Almost a year had gone by when Al found himself in a tough place, the recipient of a very serious personnel complaint for unprofessional behavior and sexual harassment. It was his first complaint since being at West Hollywood. A female motorist had received a ticket from Al, as he worked a one-man patrol car.

She was cited for going 50 mph in a 30-mph zone. In the car with the woman during the incident was her daughter, a girl who was about twelve years old.

The written complaint accused Al of lying about the speed, calling the motorist a lousy, rich bitch and suggesting that the ticket would not be issued if the woman spent some time relieving Al's frustrations and desires in the back seat of the patrol car. The twelve-year-old girl confirmed the validity of the complaint. Additionally, the woman had contacted both a lawyer and the local newspaper in which her allegations and the story had been given front-page coverage.

The complaint had been received by the Internal Investigations Bureau on a Saturday morning and a Commander who was responsible for Department operations on the weekend had ordered Al relieved of duty, pending the outcome of an investigation.

Once again, Al found himself facing a lieutenant who was informing him that his alleged conduct did not meet the standard set by the Department only now he was relieved of his law enforcement duties. He was directed to go home and to be available by telephone during daytime business hours. Al handed over his badge, identification and pistol and left the station feeling that his world was ending.

"It's bullshit," he said to himself. "It never happened."

Later, he talked to a Union Representative, who was in the process of arranging an interview with a Union Lawyer to whom Al would tell his side of the story. Once home, it turned out to be an incredibly long day for him. He tried to read and watch television but he couldn't stay focused on either. His mind kept drifting back to the situation he was in and he was worried. It didn't help when the phone rang and as he answered it, he hoped it wasn't somebody from Internal Investigations.

"Hello?"

"Hi Al, this is Odie, got a minute?"

"Yes sir."

"I'd like to come over in a couple minutes and talk to you off the record. You don't have to if you don't want to and you can have a Union Representative with you if you want."

"Ya, O.K., but I'm taking you at your word that it's off the record."

"I'll be there in five minutes."

Al saw Odie's black, 4 door, Department owned, Ford Crown Victoria pull up in front and he watched as the big man navigated the steps up the walkway to the front door.

They exchanged pleasantries as Al invited him into the small, neat living room of his West L.A. condo. "I've got coffee, if you'd like."

"Sounds good, black please."

A few minutes later they were facing each other, Odie on the couch and Al in his recliner. Odie sipped his coffee and then muttered something about how it wasn't too bad for a bachelor to have made. Al forced a grin.

"I'm not going to be here long or try to B.S. you- you're in a tough spot right now and you don't need somebody like me to make it worse. I'm only going to ask you one, well, maybe two questions.

Do you remember the two things I told you I wanted from you when you got to the Station?

"Yes, I do."

"O.K., here's the big question, based on those two things, have we got anything to worry about- and you might want to think for a minute before you answer me?

"Captain, I don't have to think about my answer, I didn't do anything out of line, what that lady says I did is 100% pure, unadulterated bull shit! Nobody at the Station and especially you, has anything to worry about."

Odie looked at Al for a long minute and then spoke, "O.K. kid, I believe you. I want to see you get exonerated; have you got any ideas about how we can show that this complaint is a crock?"

"Just one thing sir."

"What's that?"

"A micro- cassette recording of the stop that's got every word I spoke and everything that lady and her kid said to me."

"No shit? Well let's hear it!"

Al played the tape for Odie and what he heard was a perfectly normal initial conversation between a traffic cop and a motorist who was being informed of the speeding violation and the intention to issue a ticket for the offense. It wasn't until the time on the tape when Al returned to the motorist's window to explain the citation: how to handle payment or appeal and to request the motorist's signature that things got strange.

"Isn't there some way to take care of this other than by getting a ticket, perhaps I could get to know you a whole lot better? You're kinda cute, even my daughter thinks so. Don't you dear?"

"He's handsome and I especially like his blue eyes."

"How about it, honey, you let me give you a little something personal and you let me go with a warning?"

"Ma'am, please sign the ticket, next to the X, it's your promise to appear, it is not an admission of guilt."

"Been here too long huh, don't like girls anymore?

"Please ma'am, just sign the ticket so we can both be on our way."

"You're nothing but a tin badged, chicken shit, asshole, I'll have you fired. We know how to fix idiots like you." There was a brief moment of silence interspersed with the sound of rustling paper and then Al spoke.

"Here's your copy ma'am, please drive safely."

"Screw you cop, your ass is mine, you'll be dead meat when I'm done with you."

Then the tape stopped.

Al looked at Odie who had a large grin on his face. "I read an article in the Sheriff's Relief Association Magazine a while back, it was on how to survive a citizen's complaint by using a voice activated micro-cassette recorder on traffic stops and such, so I decided to buy one."

"Well Al, I think you just got your money's worth out of the purchase, that tape is worth more than its weight in gold. For God's sake don't let anything happen to it." If it's O.K. with you,

I'd like to turn up the heat on the Internal Investigations Bureau so that this thing gets moved along so you can come back to work.

The other thing I'd like to see happen is for this complainant to hang herself out all the way. We should have a solid criminal case against her for filing a false police report. If she sues you and the Department maybe we can have the D.A. use that as a second offense.

I'm glad you agreed to talk to me Al, you've made my day and probably my year!"

"Thanks Captain, I really appreciate you taking the time with me.

I wasn't really happy when I came here from Firestone Station, I thought I'd been given the shaft, but you couldn't have treated me any better, the troops say you're a standup guy and they weren't wrong."

Al found himself returned to duty in less than two days. He was kept advised of the proceedings involving the complainant and was surprised when Odie told him that she had been arrested and booked for filing a false police report. The local press had the story and used it, although it didn't show up on the front page.

"Al, you're a good Deputy, I hope you realize that the Department takes the kind of complaint made against you very seriously. On the other hand, we want to make absolutely certain that you get a fair shake and when you help us prove your innocence, we're happy as hell. Good job!

By the way, when I stopped by your place, I noticed the flag in the presentation case, did you have a family member who was a casualty in the service?"

"No, I was working the Desk at Firestone Station on the night it was shut down, that's the flag that flew there on that day. I kept it to remind me of that place."

"I worked at Firestone Station too, I was a Deputy and a Sergeant there, I liked the ride."

The next months went by swiftly, Al had gained a little more stature at the Station as a result of having weathered a personal storm and having come out on top.

Odie continued to be a good Station Captain, the City loved him, the community was happy and his troops saw him as somebody who looked out for them on and off the job. His people off sick or with family emergencies got personal visits and phone calls and genuine offers of help and support. He was known as somebody who sincerely cared about the people who worked with him.

The intention was to issue a ticket for the offense. It wasn't until the time on the tape when Al returned to the motorist's window to explain the citation: how to handle payment or appeal and to request the motorist's signature that things got strange.

"Isn't there some way to take care of this other than by getting a ticket, perhaps I could get to know you a whole lot better? You're kinda cute, even my daughter thinks so. Don't you dear?"

"He's handsome and I especially like his blue eyes."

"How about it, honey, you let me give you a little something personal and you let me go with a warning?"

"Ma'am, please sign the ticket, next to the X, it's your promise to appear, it is not an admission of guilt."

"Been here too long huh, don't like girls anymore?

"Please ma'am, just sign the ticket so we can both be on our way."

"You're nothing but a tin badged, chicken shit, asshole, I'll have you fired. We know how to fix idiots like you."

There was a brief moment of silence interspersed with the sound of rustling paper and then Al spoke.

"Here's your copy ma'am, please drive safely."

"Screw you cop, your ass is mine, you'll be dead meat when I'm done with you."

Then the tape stopped.

Al looked at Odie who had a large grin on his face. "I read an article in the Sheriff's Relief Association Magazine a while back, it was on how to survive a citizen's complaint by using a voice activated micro-cassette recorder on traffic stops and such, so I decided to buy one."

"Well Al, I think you just got your money's worth out of the purchase, that tape is worth more than its weight in gold. For God's sake don't let anything happen to it." If it's O.K. with you,

I'd like to turn up the heat on the Internal Investigations Bureau so that this thing gets moved along so you can come back to work.

The other thing I'd like to see happen is for this complainant to hang herself out all the way. We should have a solid criminal case against her for filing a false police report. If she sues you and the Department maybe we can have the D.A. use that as a second offense.

I'm glad you agreed to talk to me Al, you've made my day and probably my year!"

"Thanks Captain, I really appreciate you taking the time with me.

I wasn't really happy when I came here from Firestone Station, I thought I'd been given the shaft, but you couldn't have treated me any better, the troops say you're a standup guy and they weren't wrong."

Al found himself returned to duty in less than two days. He was kept advised of the proceedings involving the complainant and was surprised when Odie told him that she had been arrested and booked for filing a false police report. The local press had the story and used it, although it didn't show up on the front page.

"Al, you're a good Deputy, I hope you realize that the Department takes the kind of complaint made against you very seriously. On the other hand, we want to make absolutely certain that you get a fair shake and when you help us prove your innocence, we're happy as hell. Good job!

By the way, when I stopped by your place, I noticed the flag in the presentation case, did you have a family member who was a casualty in the service?"

"No, I was working the Desk at Firestone Station on the night it was shut down, that's the flag that flew there on that day. I kept it to remind me of that place."

"I worked at Firestone Station too, I was a Deputy and a Sergeant there, I liked the ride."

The next months went by swiftly, Al had gained a little more stature at the Station as a result of having weathered a personal storm and having come out on top.

Odie continued to be a good Station Captain, the City loved him, the community was happy and his troops saw him as somebody who looked out for them on and off the job. His people off sick or with family emergencies got personal visits and phone calls and genuine offers of help and support. He was known as somebody who sincerely cared about the people who worked with him.

The idea of Odie leaving the Department was something that caught the people at West Hollywood Station unaware.

For a short time, the Station buzzed with rumors: that although he was old enough to retire, he had a mysterious illness that was forcing the issue; a rich relative had left him a huge inheritance; He'd met and fallen in love with a girl in Tahiti. It wasn't long before Odie attended the various shift briefings and he put the rumors to rest and explained the reason for his pending retirement.

"The City of West Hollywood has offered me a job as the Director of Public Safety. In short, I'll be drawing two nice paychecks, one from my retirement and the other from the City. I'll work here for a few more years and then I'll be financially secure for the rest of my life. It's an offer I can't turn down. Besides it will give me an opportunity to keep an eye on the troops here at West Hollywood Station."

Al was sad to hear Odie speak of leaving. He'd made a real difference in his career. His personal welcoming had awakened

a sense of order and direction in Al and he had benefited from those words as he took them to heart. - Be honest and do a good job. He wondered if there were many other Captains who'd come over to your house and sit down with you and try to figure out a way out of a tough spot. He didn't think there were. "He likes the troops and they like and respect him," Al thought.

As usual for a well-liked Captain, there was a big retirement party with hundreds of well-wishers. There were a lot of awards and presentations for Odie from the Department and allied organizations. Although Al wasn't on the program, he'd brought something for Odie that he thought the Captain might like to have.

As the evening wore on, Commander Bill Mc Sweeny, the Master of Ceremonies was in the process of bringing the event to a close and that's when Al got to his feet and made his way forward with his present.

"I got one more thing to give him," Al said in a voice that was starting to choke up.

Mc Sweeny called the program back to order and the hundreds of guests retook their seats, wondering what the young man at the microphone and podium was going to do.

Al had a tough time talking, he hadn't intended it to happen, it just did. His voice quavered and broke with emotion as he spoke about Odie, the man who had helped him and probably had saved his career, a guy that the troops loved and respected because they knew he cared about them. Those who were listening were aware that Al was speaking from his heart and that he was trying his best to do something meaningful for the man they honored this night.

"Captain," he said as he opened a large brown paper bag, I took this flag home with me on the night that Firestone Station closed for the last time. I think it's very special. I wanted to give it to you for saving my job and I know you worked at Firestone for a long time and I think that it would be a good thing if you had this. Thanks for all you did for me and everybody else, I want you to have The Colors."

For a moment there was silence from the audience and then, in unison, those assembled came to their feet and wave after wave of applause echoed through the room as Al and Odie stood together.

Odie held the flag case in one arm and the other was around the shoulder of one of his troops. Many of those who watched were thinking to themselves that there could not have been a finer closing or tribute to a career well spent.

The tattered and worn flag, dressed up in the glass and wooden presentation case didn't make the flashy impression that the other awards had made, those from the desk of a politician, agency head or organization. The others were momentos and tokens that couldn't compare or match this Presentation of Colors, a torn and worn flag that meant much to those assembled, the man giving it and the man receiving it. It was one of those once in a lifetime moment forever treasured. It was a gift that had come after thoughtful reflection and it came from the heart.

Odie had teared up a little and he too was having difficulty getting his words out. All he could say as the evening came to a very special close was, "Thanks Al, I'll keep and treasure these Colors forever."

THE CRIME FIGHTERS

By, Assist Sheriff, Duane Preimsberger, retired

At a little after nine on a Friday evening, Pumpkin Head and the Turkey were seated next to each other on maroon, Naugahyde covered wooden bar stools in the dimly, lit, smoky cave known as O'Leary's Bar and Grill. A couple of five-dollar bills occupied a space between their bottles of Guinness Stout, the wager between the two of them over where O'Leary would land.

"Mashed potatoes, mashed potatoes, come on mashed potatoes!" encouraged the Turkey.

"No way!" argued Pumpkin Head, "he's going to land in the peas."

The proprietor of this less than classy establishment, 60-year-old Patrick Francis O'Leary, was on the nod in one of the small booths that matched the barstools. In front of him, on the red checkered, oil-cloth covered table was a plate of roast beef, mashed potatoes, brown gravy and peas. O'Leary's head continued to make its barely perceptible, downward passage toward the slowly growing cold contents of the plate. The event was accompanied by the sounds of O'Leary's snoring and the Irish Rovers singing, "Danny Boy," coming from the See burg Juke Box.

Margaret Shaughnessy, an elderly regular at O'Leary's sat several stools away from Pumpkin Head. She too was drinking Guinness, her 8th or 9th bottle of the evening.

Her speech was difficult to understand, not only because of her alcohol level, but also because, as usual at this hour of the evening, Margaret had removed her upper and lower dentures and was giving them "an air" on the bar top, where they grimaced back at Pumpkin Head.

"Donamakefun ahim," she slurred, "HezaO.K.guy, usta be mysqueeze!!"

"Put your teeth back in Margaret, them things are giving me the creeps sitting there grinning at me. We're not making fun of O'Leary; we've got a very proper, honorable and gentlemanly wager on where he's going to land on his plate. As a matter of fact, as soon as he lands in the peas and I pick up the ten bucks, I'll buy you another bottle."

"Imustamisunnerstood," gummed Margaret as a lovely Irish smile appeared on her toothless countenance. "S'cuseme."

"No offense taken, me dear," replied Pumpkin Head.

O'Leary's head finally came to an abrupt rest on the plate, his nose went into the mashed potatoes and gravy while his forehead hit the peas. He twitched around for a couple of seconds and then inhaled some of the contents of the plate and began gasping and coughing. As he sat up in the booth, he gave his head a couple of hard shakes, creating a mini-shower of peas and face smashed potatoes and gravy.

"Winner, winner, as usual I'm a winner," laughed the Turkey, "barkeep, another round for me and my two friends and see if O'Leary wants something to clear his palate."

"He hit the peas first," argued Pumpkin Head.

"Bullshit," replied the Turkey, "O'Leary's got one of the biggest beezers in all of Los Angeles County. That thing hit a full second before his forehead ever touched the peas."

"Ya, you're probably right. OK."

The two of them watched as Margaret, armed with a stack of paper bar napkins, tried to clean up the semi-awake O'Leary while she crooned along with the next juke box selection. "Keepaeye on myteeth," she ordered in between choruses.

Pumpkin Head had a real name; he was baptized Darryl Thomas Horton almost forty years ago and his partner, the Turkey was, in fact, James Keith.

The two of them had gone through the Los Angeles County Sheriff's Academy together over fifteen years ago. They had shared the same assignments throughout their careers. They'd worked among the winos, thieves and wife beaters at the Hall of Justice Jail in downtown, then on to Norwalk Station as patrol deputies, policing a mostly middle-class community. Together, they had transferred to the Special Enforcement Bureau, a mobile, highly skilled and well-trained unit. S.E.B. worked specialized assignments and high crime problem areas, when requested, across Los Angeles County.

They were both Sergeants now, assigned to the Detective Bureau at Firestone Station, in South-Central L.A., as partners. Their families had become intertwined in their careers and were fast friends. They had shared vacations, backyard barbecues, birthdays and graduations. Pumpkin Head and Turkey were partners, on and off the job.

They had been given the nicknames at the Special Enforcement Bureau after their initiation, "baptism," which entailed being thrown, fully clothed into a rather slimy, duck pond that was adjacent to the Bureau facility. This rite of passage had begun years ago and the baptism meant acceptance into the Bureau as a full-fledged member.

Pumpkin Head was a stocky man, he had a very short neck and his head was probably 20% larger than average. During late October, one of the sarcastic wags at S.E.B. had suggested that since he hadn't had time to buy a Halloween pumpkin that perhaps Darryl would agree to sit on his front porch with a candle in his mouth. "With a head that size, you'd do just great as a makeshift Jack o'Lantern; how about it, Pumpkin Head?"

Turkey, although not skinny, had a wattle neck and sharper features. He was over 6 feet tall and walked with an unusual gait that resembled, to a slight degree, that of the barnyard fowl he came to be named after. What really cemented it, however, was a high-risk warrant service, where the Special Enforcement Bureau was used as the entry team. The location was in a rural area where there was a large barnyard. After the operation had been concluded and the bad guy had been taken into custody, the sun was coming up over the horizon and the birds, including turkeys, began to parade in their pen.

"Jim, your relatives are awake and they want to say hello," coming from an anonymous voice- that was all it took. Pumpkin Head and Turkey had been given their nicknames.

"Margaret, here's a handful of quarters, keep the music coming, OK?" Turkey

asked, as he slid the change down the bar where it stopped just short of her teeth.

"I'm in the wind as soon as I finish this one," said Pumpkin Head.

"Me too."

Bottles emptied, the two partners gave Margaret, the bartender and O'Leary a wave goodnight and went out the back door into the parking lot. They exchanged; "see ya Monday morning," and then the two partners went off to their homes and families.

On Monday, they both arrived at Firestone Station Detective Bureau around 8:15. Together, they looked at the In-Custody Log to determine if they had anybody to interview in the Station Jail who had been busted over the weekend hours for suspicion of robbery or assault or some other crime against a person.

They worked those kinds of cases, however, this morning they were clear of in custodies, all the bad guys had either bailed out or had been transferred to the main jail.

"I'll read the crime reports," volunteered Pumpkin Head, taking a stack of paperwork from a metal tray marked "Crimes Against Persons" with a Dyno label. "You get the coffee."

"Deal."

"Oh Shit!" Pumpkin Head said to no one in particular as he turned the pages of a crime report, "this guy's got a real problem."

The Turkey approached; carrying two steaming mugs, each emblazoned with a gold and blue Sheriff's star and their nicknames in gold script. "Got anything good?"

"Got something weird, there's a young, white guy who's flashing women in laundromats. Apparently, he hides in the restroom until he's got an audience and then he leaps out at them, fully exposed, dances around, up, on and over the machines and then he's out the door."

"O.K., in most parts of town that might be weird, but this is here. Is there something else?"

"Well, perhaps a small item. This guy is naked except for a blue cape, short black boots and a Lone Ranger style eye mask. He sprays his private parts with some kind of glittery gold stuff and has red, white and blue lightning bolts arcing away from his Mr. Johnson."

"Like I said, what's the weird part?"

"This is the fifth report in 3 days and you know there's got to be more where the victims are too flustered to talk to the cops about this kind of thing.

But the worst part about this is that the local newspaper has gotten wind of this and you know they'll want to know what we're doing.

The desk man on the morning watch left us a note saying that a news guy read the press board early this morning and was asking about these cases."

"Well, we'd better tell our Lieutenant so he can brief up the Captain then he won't get blindsided if somebody calls. Since you got the details from the report you do the talking and I'll just look pretty."

"O.K., before we go in let's make some quick calls to the adjoining police departments and see if they have any more info on like cases and maybe want to team up to catch this guy. Then we can get a list of the area laundromats from the Yellow Pages and try to figure out where our Caped Crude Satyr will go next."

"Wow, that's why I love you so much, Pumpkin darling, you're actually going to make us look good, well prepared and knowledgeable, I'm impressed."

"Ya, I know and when we lay this on em, just forget about the looking pretty part, we're talking about you."

"Hey! Margaret likes me! She thinks I'm a hunk!"

After a half dozen calls, the two partners had found two more cases and had garnered the support of a Detective from Police Departments in the cities of Huntington Park, Maywood, Bell and South Gate to help them stakeout their flasher. They used red grease pencil on a plastic covered, 8 ½"x 11", reporting district map to mark and identify the locations of the incidents in sequence and by time of day. Then they walked into the Detective Lieutenant's office.

"Happy Monday, L.- T., we've got something that's going to make your day."

Pumpkin addressed Lieutenant Preimsberger, a taciturn man, who sat at his desk reading statistical information from an F.B.I. yearly crime report and staring at the two of them from over the top of his Ben Franklin, half glasses.

"What the hell do you two want?"

Pumpkin Head ran down the information they had gathered and showed him the marked-up reporting district map for reference as he talked.

"Well, tell me what you're going to do to put this clown in jail, so I can brief the Captain?"

"Well, L.-T., as you can see, he hits regularly, at about 6 A.M. so we're going to use some guys from the local P.D.s and the two of us for a few days to sit on the local laundromats he hasn't hit yet. Maybe we'll get lucky and catch him in the act. We're going to start tomorrow morning. All we need from you is an O.K. to check out some wheels from the surveillance motor pool."

"You've got my approval, keep me informed." Lt. P-berger said as he gathered up the marked-up reporting district map. "I'll have this back to you after I run this by the Boss."

By noon the two partners had three target laundromats identified, and had given the responsibility for the two in other jurisdictions to the assisting cop's teams. They'd sit on the one in their area in a dented, faded blue and primer colored, 65 Ford, pick-up truck, complete with a rusty shell and gardening equipment in the backend. On the way back from the surveillance motor pool, Turkey had dropped off a couple of the Sheriff's tactical radios at the Police Departments so that they and their assisting cops could talk to each other during the operation.

On Tuesday morning, at 4:45, all of the guys involved in their surveillance met at Firestone Station. They had coffee and day-old Dolly Madison Bakery sweet rolls while Pumpkin Head and Turkey gave them a quick briefing on all they'd learned. By 5:20 the three teams were in route to their assigned laundromats.

The nasty looking Ford pick-up, with its rebuilt engine, transmission and suspension purred along the awakening area streets, with Pumpkin Head at the wheel. They parked as unobtrusively as possible in the parking lot of a 24-hour supermarket parking lot across the street from their empty laundromat in the 2200 block of east Florence Avenue. They had a good view of the interior of the place and were pleased to see that it didn't have a rear exit.

They settled in and watched as the sun slowly crept into view to the east and began to focus its rays on the automatic sensors that turned off the yellow tinged streetlights.

"Second pass from the blue Volkswagen bug," said the Turkey. "He's looking in the window of the place, scoping it out, could be our guy."

"Yup, here he comes again," replied Pumpkin Head as he hit the floor mounted radio button with his foot and talked into the sun-visor microphone. "Location One to Two and Three, we've got a possible, cruising our spot, he's on his third pass in a blue V.W."

"10-4, keep us advised."

The V.W. made a U-turn and parked in front of the laundromat, just past the front door. Turkey and Pumpkin Head looked on as the lone occupant and driver slid into the passenger seat, then out the door and into the restroom of the facility. His blue cape flapping behind him.

"Location One to Two and Three, our suspect just entered our location. He's in the blue cape mode and has gone inside to the head. Can you roll and take up locations directly east and west of our spot?

"10-4 this is Two, we'll take the east in two minutes."

"This is Three we got the west, in about two as well."

In a few minutes, all three teams were set up and ready as two young Mexican women walked toward the establishment. One of them was pushing a baby stroller containing two small children. The second woman pushed a supermarket-shopping cart loaded with dirty clothing while a toddler lurched along the sidewalk beside her.

"This is Two, possible victims just passed us."

"10-4."

"10-4."

Minutes passed after the women entered and began to load several of the washing machines with the clothes from the shopping cart as they got the wash started. They had seated themselves next to each other, facing the machines, in the well-worn chrome and plastic chairs against the wall when the door on the restroom cracked open.

"This is One, get ready, the restroom door just opened and we think our flashers about to dash. Two, make sure he doesn't get to his car, we don't want this to go mobile."

"Two, 10-4." Following the response two cops in plainclothes sauntered to a spot at the front of the parked Volkswagen.

Pumpkin Head and Turkey were out of the truck and moving across the street as they watched in near disbelief as the young suspect leapt from the restroom to atop the washing machines, dancing, waving his cape and screaming, "I'm Super Dong, I'm super hung, gaze upon my golden love stick, you whores."

He did a brief bump and grind and was off the machines and out the front door while the expression of shock was still appearing on the faces of the two women.

For a naked guy with a cape he moved pretty good and in a matter of a millisecond he'd identified the guys closing in on him as cops, and the foot chase was on. Turkey had been a middling track and field jock in high school and junior college and he quickly outdistanced the other pursuers.

The caped guy had about a 15-yard lead as they raced down an alley toward an eight-foot tall, chain linked, barbed wire topped gate and Turkey watched in amazement as the cape came off and was thrown over the top of the barbed wire.

Suddenly the naked man scampered up the gate made an improbable pole vault styled leap, up and over the top and then as he landed on his feet, he ran into the area's residential back yards.

Turkey could hear the neighborhood dogs barking as the guy fled from them.

Seconds later he was joined by five puffing, out of breath, Detectives who seemed to ask all at once, "Where'd he go?"

Pumpkin Head, breathing hard, was on his handheld radio asking for uniformed officer assistance and black and white patrol cars to help track the naked guy down and four units acknowledged that they were on the way. One of them was a unit with a search dog.

"He jumped the fence like some sort of naked pole vaulter, he did leave his cape as a souvenir. It's up there on the barbed wire. First time I've ever competed against a masked guy with golden privates, I'd be amazed if I ever forget the sight of him going over that gate, it was almost patriotic with that red, white and blue stuff waving in the breeze, I shoulda saluted."

"Let's get back to our wheels and help look for this mope, except you guys in Two, maybe you could impound the V.W. for us and get the names and horse powers of the victims?"

"Sure thing."

The station dispatcher beeped the frequency and began a broadcast. "Attention Firestone units involved in the search, see the woman at 2301 E. Flower Street, she reports a naked man is hiding in her dog house in the backyard. Any unit to respond in two or less, identify?"

The first response came from the canine unit; it had an ETA of under one-minute.

"Hell," said Turkey, "he's right behind us. Flower Street is the next block south so he's got to be in a yard real close. We can probably find him just by looking over the fences."

Within a few seconds they were looking into a small, neat back yard where an old, graying, mongrel dog sat on its haunches, staring at its doghouse and barking a slow tired bark at whatever or whoever was inside.

They pushed open the alley gate and entered the yard as the old dog turned his attention to them and the back door of the house flew open. An elderly woman squinted at them while asking in a quavering voice, "Are you the police?"

"Yes ma'am," Turkey responded as he held his badge up for her to see.

"Well, I can see somebody's naked fanny in that dog house and Killer has been barking at it. I hope you'll take 'em out of here, this scares me and I've got a bad heart."

"We'll have this taken care of in a few minutes, ma'am."

Deputy Roosevelt Jones came through the side gate with a leashed Rottweiler at his side that was the size and bulk of a small bedroom dresser.

"What you guys got," he asked.

Turkey told him and Roosevelt smiled and said, "Bruno and I would be pleased to help get him out if you want."

"Sounds good to us."

Roosevelt took Bruno to the side of the dog house and spoke a few commands in Danish to the dog who immediately changed from a docile animal into a raging, snarling, growling, evil intentioned beast who bit and shook the dog house for a few moments.

Roosevelt issued another Danish command and the transformation reversed as Bruno sat down by the deputy's side with his stumpy tail wagging in the grass.

Killer, the old dog, had retreated to the steps leading to the back door and was scratching hard at it, trying to get inside and away from the demonstration of evil he had just witnessed.

"Holy shit," muttered Pumpkin Head, "I'm glad Bruno's on our side."

"If you don't come out of there with your hands out in front of you where we can see them, I'm going to let my dog go in there and he'll bring you out and I guarantee you won't like that very much. Do you hear me?"

O.K., O.K., I'm coming out, just don't let him bite me!!" came the timid voiced reply from within the doghouse.

Seconds later, a scared, pimply faced, thin, young man emerged from the dog house, trying to hold his hands in view while at the same time concealing his glittering private parts and lightning bolt embellished stomach and thighs from view. "I give up," he whispered.

Pumpkin Head handcuffed him and then pulled an old dog blanket from the doghouse and draped it around the kid. "Hold onto the end of this, we don't want you scaring anybody else with your art work."

They were busy for a few minutes; retrieving the cape, returning the dog blanket, getting the victim info, doing the vehicle impound paperwork and offering thanks all around to the other Detectives and the uniformed Deputies. Then Pumpkin Head and Turkey loaded Super Dong into the middle seat in the pick-up truck, put new blanket around him and drove to Firestone Station with their prisoner.

They photographed him in his Super Dong outfit, then fingerprinted and booked him into the jail system and gave him some orange coveralls with L.A. County Jail, stenciled on the front and back. After that, they took him to a small interrogation room and began to interview him as Turkey read him the Miranda Rights admonition.

Roger William Lynn was 19 years old, an unemployed local resident who lived with his folks. He was a registered sex offender and had several arrests for exposing himself to grammar school kids. He was on Probation and had been committed for a short time to a State Mental Hospital for evaluation and treatment.

He was presently a psychiatric outpatient and was on medication. However, he didn't like the shape and color of the new pills he'd recently been given so he had stopped taking them a week before the laundromat incidents had begun.

"They are yucky, they look like bird droppings and I ain't putting them in my mouth anymore."

The cape was in reality, a dark blue, terrycloth bathrobe with the sleeves cut off and a big Superman emblem on the back, it had been a birthday present from his mom. The gold glitter and red, white and blue decoration had been purchased in a local arts and crafts store and applied with tender, loving care to his Mr. Johnson and surrounding areas.

"I'm sort of an artist, ya know? I like to make my thing pretty! Do you like it?"

"That's it," Pumpkin Head said grumpily to Turkey, "I'm getting us a cup of coffee. You talk to Rembrandt here about his paintings, maybe we can schedule him as an exhibit at one of them art galleries on the west side."

"Oh my! Wouldn't that be wonderful, then even more people could see my beautiful, huge, sex machine."

Pumpkin Head slammed the interrogation room door as he left, shaking his head.

It was early afternoon before they were finished with the paperwork, phone calls to Roger's Probation Officer, a visit to the District Attorney's Office and a briefing with our Lieutenant.

"O.K. L.- T., this is a wrap, we got the guy, his P.O. has a hold on him and is going to make arrangements to send him back to the wacko ward. The D.A. at San Antonio Court gave us a wienie waver filing, so if and when Super Dong gets well, we can give him another shot at jail." Pumpkin Head said.

"Well it ain't quite a wrap, today must be a slow news day so a couple of TV crews are going to show up here to film somebody telling them how we managed to nail this guy and stop the terrification of our female population.

The Captain and I can't think of two better victims than you guys. Handle it."

"O.K. pretty boy," Pumpkin said. "This is your chance to star, maybe Margaret will see you and ask for your autograph the next time you're in O'Leary's."

"All right, I'll do it. Got any hair spray?"

Later, as Turkey walked from his car in the driveway at home, the back door opened and his seven-year-old son, James Jr., exploded out of it, running hard as he approached.

"Daddy, daddy!! You and Mr. Pumpkin are famous! Me and mom just watched you guys on the news, you were great! The lady says your real crime fighters and that you caught a bad man who was scaring ladies and put him in jail!"

As Jimmy hugged him the Turkey smiled and replied as he hugged him back, "and you're a real kid and I'm glad you're mine. Now let's see what mom's got for dinner for her favorite crime fighter."

LOVE-ET' KAYPULLS

A LOOK AT THE PAST REMEMBER?

By Duane Preimsberger, Asst. Sheriff, retired

One of the greatest rewards of being retired members of the Los Angeles County Sheriff's Department comes from the memories of our service. The recognition that we worked in an organization that truly strived to make

Los Angeles County a better place will always be with us. We struggled to make a positive difference and sometimes it was enormous and other times it was small but we tried every day that we served. As we look back over the years and remember, I believe that all of us are touched by the recognition of how fortunate we were to be a part of the Department. In those moments of recollection, we recognize that we took away perhaps more than we gave. It was a real honor to be a part of a proud and noble organization, one that managed to make its community just a little better. It was a collective effort one that Sheriff's through the years have called the work of a family and perhaps it was so.

The recollections that I write about are not mine. They are the collective remembrances of dozens of men and women who served through the years. I've received tidbits over time and although I couldn't use all of them because of space constraints there are some folks who deserve special recognition for their efforts and I apologize in advance if I've forgotten anyone.

Joining the LASD in the 50's and 60's and into the 70's was different. After you were hired in on the second floor of the Hall of Justice, a clerk swore you in and then you got a briefing from somebody important about not having your new, bright and shiny badge around. You got an explicit explanation about what those six points would do if somebody shoved it up an unmentionable portion of your anatomy. Then you got some info on where you could go to buy your uniforms, leather gear, gun, handcuffs, baton, sap and rain gear. Because there wasn't any free safety equipment, you paid for it yourself. Most new hires walked down to Sam Cooks near the Garment District and signed up for time payments for the stuff and listened to an endless sales pitch about the need for an off-duty gun and so forth from Sam or one of the staff. After the tailors sewed all the patches on and tailored it, you raced home, put it on and swaggered around the house looking in the mirrors to see if you were as intimidating as the cops you'd seen in the movies. At some point in time you took out the straight, hardwood baton with the leather thong and tried to spin it like the foot beat cops in New York. This exercise invariably led to a smack on the elbow or worse yet breaking a lamp or Aunt Tillie's wedding gift vase.

The fun had just begun, next you got to report to the Academy at Bacillus Center where people called Drill Instructors stood nose to nose with you and harangued on about what a ridiculous excuse for a human being you were. Since they were so loud and intimidating you had no choice but to agree with them. The torture, based upon military boot camp, went on for as long as 16 weeks for male cadets. Females were allowed to escape to the women's jail on the 13th floor of the Hall of Justice or the women's facility on Terminal Island near the fish cannery after 10 weeks or less. It wasn't until later that Sybil Brand Institute opened.

By the time graduation rolled around you'd done thousands of push-ups next to the large replica of a badge on the ground on the Grinder. You'd run hundreds of miles through the streets of East L.A. and become very well acquainted with the snake pit, a smoldering, earthen covered dump that was adjacent to the training site. It constantly belched smelly, noxious fumes and made weird noises. It was in the snake pit that the chin-up bars and other primitive athletic equipment had been located for the entertainment of the staff and cadets.

There were two classrooms. The smaller was underneath the pistol range and to get there you had to walk below the target turning area or the pit as the Drill Instructors called it. While walking to that classroom it wasn't unusual to hear a round strike the metal target holders a few feet above your head. The larger classroom was in the Gym; a raised stage and podium stood at the west end, under a basketball backboard and the staff had desks across the back. There were lockers for the males along both sides; females were allowed a tiny room at the east end of the building. These lockers became very familiar especially in the late afternoon, when stress training came into full play and we often got to perform a drill called Switchee-Changee. One of the Drill Instructors would identify a minor imperfection that would indicate to the staff that the class was not together and not operating as a team.

To correct this, the class would be called to attention and then told to get ready for Physical Training in 5 minutes. Bedlam would occur as 100 or so cadets raced from their student desks to their lockers that were shared with one other person. They'd strip off their khaki colored uniforms, try to hang them up and get into P.T. gear and report at attention on the Grinder in the allotted time. It was almost impossible to meet the challenge, so the staff would order the cadet's back into their uniforms and the process would be repeated, over and over. A member of the staff would approach a struggling, sweat drenched cadet in the throes of getting dressed and ask a series of questions which meant that the cadet had to stop dressing, come to attention and reply. This little game could go on and on until by some miracle we managed to do it to the alleged satisfaction of the staff. Invariably, at least one Cadet would leave the Switchee-Changee drill with a ruined, torn portion of his or her uniform.

In-house instructors almost always did the training and for the most part they were good, although Don Motander from the Crime Lab was a fascinating lecturer who dazzled the Cadets by displaying over a dozen deadly weapons that he'd hidden on his slender frame. Less exciting was a nurse from County General Hospital who lectured for 3 hours in a monotone voice about the Emergency Aspects of Childbirth. If you had a desk toward the back you could watch the heads forward of you nod and snap back up to awake as she droned on. One of the few places that stress wasn't allowed was at the range, the Firearms Instructors didn't want some revved-up Cadet making a foolish mistake with a live round. One of their most difficult jobs was teaching us how to quickly reload a revolver from a dump ammo pouch: there were no speedy loaders or semi-automatic pistols.

At graduation, if you were the honor cadet you got to go straight to patrol. Otherwise you went to either the Jail Division that ran the Booking Office, Hall of Justice Jail and the Women's facility at Terminal Island or you went to the Corrections Division. Bacillus Center, the Honor Farm, Mira Loma, the Drunk Farm and the Road Camps were part of Corrections. It was easy to tell where a Deputy was assigned by his uniform: The Jail Deputies wore green and later tan and green and the Corrections Deputies wore cotton khaki uniforms. Uniformed Female Deputies wore white blouses, green skirts, girdles, full slip, nylons, raised heel pumps and a little brimless cap and carried a black shoulder strap purse containing a revolver and handcuffs.

If you really wanted to get out of your custody assignment early you requested a transfer to Patrol Main Office or PMO. This assignment was a man power pool located in the Hall of Justice that did jobs that included prisoner transportation, bailiff duties and the Mental Health Detail that went around picking up psychos. Many of the buses in those days had a three-man crew and the least senior Deputy rode in a "shotgun" cage over the rear wheels above the end of the exhaust pipe. Although separated by a wire mesh screen from the inmates, this Deputy got to enjoy exhaust odors and the smells of 50+ sometimes-unwashed prisoners. The cage wasn't air-conditioned and, in the summer, it was hot and, in the winter, it could get pretty cold.

Periodically, while waiting in the PMO bullpen for an assignment a Deputy would get drafted to go on a psycho run. Two male Deputies would be assigned to apprehend a male patient and two male Deputies and a female Deputy would track down female patients.

Sometimes the apprehensions of these individuals were more than just a little dangerous and since there weren't radios in the Mental Health Detail cars getting assistance was often difficult. Pay phones and screaming often did the job. It wasn't hard to tell the losers as they walked back in the bullpen in torn and tattered uniforms.

Uniforms for Deputies, other than those assigned to Corrections were initially all green and later a tan shirt replaced the green one. An eight-pointed, short visor green cap was a necessity whenever a Deputy was outside and if you didn't wear it on traffic stops and so forth and a supervisor saw you, you'd be reprimanded. Helmets came after the Watts Riots of 1965, until then the only unit that had them issued was SED (Special Enforcement Detail) and they displayed these all white helmets mounted on wire coat hangers in the back windows of their patrol cars. When green shirts were in vogue Deputies wore a shoulder strap to help support their Sam Browne. It wasn't a popular piece of equipment and if you got into a struggle it could be used as a suitcase handle to toss you around, especially if you were grabbed from behind. Clip on ties were in a necessity as well as wire collar stays. There was a thin, Eisenhower jacket for both men and women that did little to keep out the cold on the Morning Watch.

Ties with tie bars or tie chains were worn all the time unless the temperature outside exceeded 85 degrees and then individual Stations could broadcast a discretionary Code 11 for their field personnel. Unfortunately, many of the 12 or 13 Stations kept their thermometers well inside a shady, covered garage so that when it reached 85 there it was probably closer to 95 degrees in the sun. When short sleeved shirts came to be part of the uniform, they couldn't be worn by anyone with tattooed arms.

Ballistic vests were unheard of except for a few WWII military issue types that were maintained in the Station armory along with solid slugs for the shotguns, snake shot for the remote area stations and the special weapons: .45 cal. Rieslings, and .30.30 lever action, saddle ring, Winchester carbines. Most of the older Deputies carried

6" revolvers while the newer Deputies went for the 4". Holsters were not standard and you could see single and double swivel, high rise, cross draw, flap, and clamshell. Saps were a common place item and included a wide range of types: beavertail, spring loaded and 3 levels of Gonzales saps made by a Deputy. They ranged in size and weight and were given designations to match; the 415, 245 and 187 models.

The 187-model looked like a small baseball bat and if carried in a trousers rear sap pocket it's handle rose to belt level.

Some personnel, particularly Detectives, carried a palm sap, it looked like a leather watch strap was running across the top of your hand while a couple of ounces of lead dust was concealed in a leather wrapped container in you palm. Slapping somebody on the ear with it was bound to get his or her immediate attention. Some detectives also carried a come along device known as the claw. The claw portion would be jammed against a wrist and then cinched down with a corkscrew handle causing deep bone pain.

Patrol cars were going through a change and we saw everything including Grey Ghosts, early 1950's vintage Fords painted solid grey with a large gold star on the front door. These six cylinders, stick shift vehicles had a six-volt electrical system. At night, if you needed to operate in a Code 3 mode you could have your choice of red lights and siren or headlights but not both at the same time, there wasn't enough juice to power both systems together. They were also unheated and if you needed to cool off you rolled down all the windows. 1957 saw the first Ford V8, an Interceptor engine that came from T-birds and could really accelerate. 1958 saw us with Chevrolets and brakes that faded completely after 4 or 5 hard applications, they made slowing down for intersections a real challenge. The black and white patrol units had two way radios any other black and whites or plain units usually didn't. Being flagged down by a citizen who needed help posed a challenge for someone in a non-radio-equipped unit. Corrections had some tan Studebaker sedans with Sheriff's stars on the door and these were driven by unit Captains.

Red lights and siren were mounted on a triangular aluminum plate that was bolted to the roof. The sirens were mechanical and took a second or two to reach audible pitch, when they started to wind up it sounded like the beginnings of the old Civil Defense air raid siren test inside the patrol car. There were two small red lights to the front and a single amber to the rear, later the red lights were replaced with two larger, thin plastic lenses, lights and these, "Mickey Mouse" ears, could be rotated so they faced sideways instead of to the front. Deputy's leaving their cars were well advised to check the position of the lights on their return to assure that a prankster hadn't re-aimed them.

Staying within radio communication was difficult without portable radios. So, the common practice upon exiting the patrol car was to turn the radio up to maximum volume and to leave the doors open so that it could be heard. The first real portables were put in use in the late 1960's and were heavy and the size of a lunch box. They had a carrying strap that went from your gun side shoulder to your opposite hip where the radio dangled. It had a whip antenna that would regularly smack door jambs, tree limbs and other objects that were a couple of feet above your head.

Air Support was pretty limited, the Aero Bureau was located in a big tin hanger on a hillside in E.L.A. above the Academy and just below the Fire Department HQ. There were 4 or 5 Bell G3B helicopters that looked like they were left- overs from the M.A.S.H. television program. They could hold 3 people and had a Stokes litter rack mounted on the top of the skid platform. One of these birds was supercharged and it was used for mountain rescue response since it had the lift required to haul victims from mountain-tops. The pilots of those days recall unconscious victims coming awake and finding himself at 3000', going 85 mph. while lying on his back and strapped in a Stokes litter hanging off the side of a tinker-toy helicopter enroute to a hospital. The look of terror on those faces was unforgettable. Air patrol operations were initiated at Lakewood Station in 1966 with the advent of Sky Knight as the Country's first municipal helicopter patrol test program. The aircraft, a small Hughes 300, was restricted to the Lakewood area except in cases of life-threatening emergencies. Lighting up areas at night was a much different operation than todays. Civilian aircraft hadn't yet developed an internally controlled illumination system so the early Sky Knight observers did things a little more unique. Aircraft mechanics and some handy Deputies built a manually operated device that held 2 or 3 landing lights on one end, followed by a pistol grip and then a brace for the observer's forearm. The observer would prop open the aircraft door with his right foot, hold onto the landing light device and then lean out of the aircraft, past the skid and light up things on the ground. It was pretty crude but it worked. Sky Knights success and operations became the urban air support model for the Nation after they improved on the light.

The Sheriff's mobile command post of the 60's looked like a bread truck that had been painted black and white. It was kept at East L.A. Station and the troops had nicknamed it the pie-wagon. It was too small and very slow and cumbersome. It's maximum speed under Code 3 conditions was below that of normal freeway speeds. The driver would continually be passed by other cars. It was used in 1965 for both the Harvey Aluminum Co. strike in Torrance and during the Watts Riots and found to be deficient at both events. It was soon replaced with real mobile command post vehicles.

Making want and warrant checks in the field or checking to determine if a vehicle was stolen was a time-consuming process that was all done by hand. A quick check of a suspect could be done in 15 to 20 minutes if you limited your inquiry to L.A.S.O. and L.A.P.D. with longer delays on busy Friday and Saturday nights.

Determining if a car was stolen was initiated by looking at the license plate on the possible stolen and then glancing up at your patrol car sun visor to see if the number was listed on the "Hot Sheet," a listing of recently stolen and wanted cars that was distribute daily by LAPD. Vehicles wanted for felonies were asterisked. If you suspected that either a subject or a vehicle was wanted in a city like Long Beach it required that someone in the radio room call there and ask that they do a hand search of their records. This process could take as long as an hour. Checks out of the immediate area or out of state were usually done by teletype.

Dispatching patrols car began when someone with a police problem called a Sheriff's station and talked to the Complaint Deputy who wrote the information down on a call sheet, time stamped it and handed it to the Dispatcher. His job was to identify a unit to handle the call and then pick up a direct phone line to Station "B", the radio room located in the Hall of Justice and voice relay the information to him a Radio Telephone Operator. "For 21, a 415, possible 242 in the street at 3rd and Eastern." A Station "B" RTO would then broadcast the call. Later after handling the incident, the bookman in 21 would call the station desk and "clear" the call. "415 over prior to arrival, unable to locate any evidence of crime. Informant Sally Ramirez F/M 42 contacted." Before going off duty the clearance would be transferred to the hand-written patrol car log and turned in at the end of watch.

The Federal Communications Commission required that every thirty minutes the broadcast frequencies in use were to be audibly identified. An RTO would start the ball rolling by asking, "any unit FCC?" The response from many units stepping on each other would be, King- Adam 4306, the call letters for the mobile unit transmitters. Some more creative minds would come up with slightly different acronyms like King-size Alligator or Kangaroo Adenoid. In any event the RTO would respond, "KMA 628, Los Angeles County Sheriff's Department clear at ___ hours."

The face of the Department was different. There was a single Patrol Division, then it was divided in Patrol East and West and finally into the three Regions. Detective Division had a Livestock Detail with experts in cattle branding. There were night detective units in the field at many stations for immediate response and follow up on major crimes. Vice Bureau was a fairly large operation with multiple crews working morals and book making. There was a Robbery Detail, a Labor Detail, and many other specialized functions that no longer exist today.

Parking enforcement was handled by Deputy Sheriff's riding 3 wheeled Harley Davidson motorcycles and that was considered to be a good job. We didn't have a Hostage Negotiator or a SWAT team until well into the 1970's.

Paramedics weren't yet invented and the Sheriff's Department was charged with handling the County Emergency Aid Program. With every request for an ambulance and every time a County fire truck left the station Code 3, a Sheriff's unit also responded. Deputies would evaluate the situation and if necessary, they'd fill out an EAP slip that authorized an ambulance to transport the victim to the hospital and to be reimbursed by the County if they couldn't collect from the patient. Since Deputies were often the first to arrive, they frequently delivered babies, or administered first-aid and CPR. Many fire companies were 3-man units so Deputies jumped in and hauled hose and helped the fire guys do their job.

Women were seeing their horizons expanded and in 1971 the Department began evaluating the possibility of permitting them to work in patrol cars. After looking around the Nation and interviewing personnel throughout the Department a decision was made to go ahead with a pilot program at several stations. In September of 1972, twelve lady Deputies and an alternate became the first women to ride in a Sheriff's patrol car. Their assignment was not universally accepted and initially there was reluctance and animosity toward their role. Some wives of male Deputies demanded that their husbands return to a Custody assignment so that they wouldn't have to work with those "home wreckers." The ladies stuck it out however and they proved themselves capable and often excellent in the job. They also managed to convince the brass to provide them with an appropriate uniform so they wouldn't be burdened with skirts, high heels and purses that weren't in the least conducive to chasing bad guys down alleys. Those pioneers set a standard of performance that's mirrored today.

The Corrections Division ran the Honor Farm when that's what it was. Crops grew there, there was a cattle herd and a dairy, a hog farm, horses, a plant nursery and a carpenter shop, where inmates could learn some skills. The Drunk Farm always had a higher population in the winter when the Skid Row derelicts decided that 3 hots and a cot was better that sleeping in a card board box under a bridge. There were Road Camps where inmates were detailed to help either the Road Department with cleanup, and construction or the Fire Department with fire break construction and maintenance and firefighting.

There were different events for personnel to work, on and off duty. The Sheriff's Rodeo raised funds for the Sheriff's Relief Association and many members of the Department volunteered their time to help put the event on.

Policing the Coliseum during football games was another event that kept people busy. A select group of Deputies and finally SED worked the Academy Awards dressed in tuxedos and providing armed security for the prestigious event. Every once in a while, a Sheriff would get a fairly serious death threat and personnel were assigned to protect him, his home and his family. The Manson Family of the late 60's and early 70's precipitated one of those months' long operations for Sheriff Peter Pitchess.

There were major and unusual occurrences to deal with and we found ourselves dealing with huge LSD parties at a time when the drug was not illegal. Responding to a loud party call at a large warehouse and finding hundreds of stoned people sometimes painting each other naked bodies with psychedelic designs while strobe lights flashed on and off the posters of Timothy Leary could be the forerunners of today's Rave events.

We responded to the tragedies of riots in Watts and East Los Angeles. Malibu had us come to fires, floods and tidal emergencies. We spent time in West Hollywood, hooking and booking, at anti-war protests and hippie demonstrations and other political upheavals. Some of us were fortunate enough to augment the Avalon troops on Catalina Island in the summer. Antelope Valley needed our help during the Hay Festivals. Firestone needed us to help police the annual Watts Summer Festivals at Will Rogers Park where Deputies made over 1000 arrests each year. The Sheriff's Countywide responsibilities saw us working with Pasadena P.D. to police the Rose Parade and Bowl games and we responded whenever another agency was overwhelmed.

As we look back with pride upon our years of service and sometimes sacrifice, we are pleased with the view. We know that we tried to help and to make a difference. It is only natural for those of us who are retired to compare those special and treasured times with the organization and its people of today. Certainly, we see many differences but there is one striking similarity and that's the willingness to help, a commitment to aid the community and each other. A Tradition of Service, long standing in an organization that is proud and honorable, the Los Angeles County Sheriff's Department. The special memories and moments are present now as they were for each of us long ago when we too were young.

THE LITTLE MOTHER

By Duane and Judy Preimsberger

It was one of those Southern California January days that passes for winter. The sky was an overcast gray and the clouds released occasional flurries of rain, the wind was bringing blasts of cold air from the northwest and had dropped the temperature into the high 40's. At eight-thirty in the morning, at least two public service agencies knew that weather was having an effect on Southern Californians.

The California Highway Patrol's incident desk was swamped with reports of traffic accidents on southland freeways. The result of light rain mixing with atmospheric sludge and oil and grease on thoroughfares created a concoction that made roadways super-slippery and motorists hurrying to work banged into each other with predictable frequency.

The second agency trying to cope with unusual demands for service was the Southern California Gas Co. Their Customer Service Reps had calls stacked up as they juggled complaints of no hot water or heat from customers who had their pilot light blown out by the strong winds. Most of them had arisen from their warm beds to find their houses "freezing" by Southern California standards, or they had climbed into the shower only to leap out, screaming invectives as the cold water hit their bodies.

Judy Preimsberger was one of a select group of locals who had reaped multiple curses from this "wintry" day. She had gotten up to find her heater wasn't working and she'd been driven from her shower by a stream of frigid water. Now she found herself gridlocked in heavy traffic caused by the rain. To make matters worse, she was fifteen minutes late for an appointment with Deputy District Attorney Art Bradley at Compton Court.

Art Bradley was perpetually unpleasant and to be inconvenienced by the tardy arrival of a cop would make him all the more difficult and Judy wasn't looking forward to their meeting. Art had been reviewing a child abuse case that Judy had brought to his office and he had sent it back with a series of questions he wanted answered before he would issue a complaint. She had the answers to those questions but she knew Bradley and she knew that she'd leave with more.

Judy was a tall, attractive, dark-haired, late thirty-something, Los Angeles County Deputy Sheriff with eleven years on the job. She had become a Deputy after learning that they made more money than did hair stylists. After surviving the rigors of Academy training and a tour at Sybil Brand Institute- the women's jail- she had transferred to East Los Angeles Station where she spent several years at the complaint desk, taking calls from the residents of East L.A. and booking any female arrestees brought to East L.A. Station by male Deputies.

She had transferred from East L.A. to Altadena Station in the foothills of the San Gabriel Mountains. She had volunteered to take part in a pilot program that placed women in patrol cars for the first time in the Departments history.

In spite of the obstacles she confronted, placed by her male co-workers who in many cases disapproved of the idea, Judy did her job well enough to gain the grudging respect of even the most vocal of the program's detractors. Several years later, she became a Station Detective, learning the ropes from seasoned investigators. She had shown more than enough competence and has managed to compete for and gain her present assignment as a Child Abuse Investigator.

"Kiddie Cops," as they were called, specialized in cases that involved the physical and sexual abuse of children, under the age of eighteen. The nature of the job was fairly complex because of the tender age of some of the victims and their intellectual capacities. It often required specialized interrogation techniques and a capacity to relate to and understand little kids, in order to draw correct information from them. Evidence gathering and courtroom presentations were often difficult because of the, very often, close relationship between the victim and the accused.

The job was stressful on occasion; dealing with broken kids who had been viciously beaten, tortured or raped, often by their caregivers; was emotionally troublesome. In spite of the downside, Judy liked her job, she enjoyed conducting in depth investigations and overcoming the difficulties in the way. Putting somebody in jail who had severely traumatized a weak, often-helpless victim gave her a sense of satisfaction. The biggest reward she got was being able to protect a small child from further vicious damage. Judy liked little kids and she was good at her job.

Her husband, Duane was a Deputy Sheriff also; the two had met a number of years ago on the job. He had ten years more experience and was an Area Commander, the rank that supervises Captains. Duane's area was a hodge-podge of four stations serving some 300,000 people in South L.A. County. The two of them were very happily married; they enjoyed each other and their life together.

Judy thought of him as she sat in the traffic jam on the northbound Long Beach Freeway. He had missed the absence of heat and hot water and the grid locked freeway this morning. Duane was attending a law enforcement seminar in Orlando, Florida. He would be home tonight and she would be there to pick him up at the airport. With any luck, he would take her to dinner on the way home and she could regale him with today's list of disasters.

She arrived at Compton Court at 9 o'clock, one half hour late for her meeting, and she surprised herself by being two minutes ahead of Art Bradley who studiously avoided commenting on the fact that he was late. Being stuck on the freeway had done little to improve his usual grumpy mood and as expected, he had more questions for

Judy to answer; to which he demanded a response within the next five working days. Their meeting, curt and abrupt had lasted less than ten minutes.

Before leaving the D.A.s office, in the court building, Judy used one of their phones to call and check in with her office. Deputy John Autrey answered the call and was pleased to hear from her.

"Glad you called," said John, "I was just about to page you. Can you respond to a Lomita Station incident and take a case from them?

They've got a nine-year-old little girl in the Pediatric Intensive Care Unit at Harbor General Hospital. She's in grave condition, none of her digestive organs are working and her other systems are failing fast. No signs of trauma and no obvious disease, the Docs think she may have been poisoned. She's been there before for a gastro-intestinal disorder, but nothing suspicious at that time. Can you meet their patrol Deputy at Harbor General?"

"I'm on the way John, I'm leaving Compton Court. E.T.A., within the next thirty minutes unless God or the C.H.P. shuts down one more freeway. I'll talk to you later." Judy hung up.

She'd been to the hospital dozens of times in the past. Harbor General had a nationally recognized Pediatrics Section and one of their specialties was handling abused and violated children and they were the primary referral hospital for an area with a population of over two million.

Judy saw a young, uniformed Deputy Sheriff seated at a desk in the police waiting room, outside the Emergency Ward of the hospital and she hoped he was her Lomita Station contact. "Hi," she said, noticing his nametag. "Deputy Knox, are you from Lomita Station?"

"Sure am. And you're from Child Abuse?"

"Right, I'm Judy Preimsberger," she said completing their introductions. "Can you fill me in on what you know?"

"Well ma'am," Knox said, showing respect to this much older woman, who had a real big head start on his twenty-four years. We got a call from the Pediatric Unit and when I got here the nurse read me a bunch of stuff from a file. Most of it was too medical for me, but what I gathered was that this little girl's insides are shot. She's probably going to die and the Docs think there's a good chance she's been poisoned. They're running more tests.

I got a chance to see her and she's a color I've never seen before on any human being, she's sort of a blue-gray all over except for eyes and they're real red. She looks like a character out of a Stephen King novel, only she's just sweet as she can be.

They've got her in a ward in the Pediatrics Section and it's just for little kids who are dying. There are seven or eight of them and they've all got all kinds of tubes and machines hooked up to them, it's kind of scary to tell you the truth, ma'am."

"Let me get some info, about the little girl, her family, where she lives, where she goes to school and how she got here?" Asked Judy.

"Got it right here in my notebook," replied Knox. "Her name is Esther Sanchez, she's nine years old, d.o.b. is 23 January 1988, born in Guatemala. Her folks have the same last name, the dad is Miguel and the Mom is Maria. She's got a five-year old brother, named Hector and a year and a half-old sister whose name is Teresa. Incidentally, they seem to be OK, Child Welfare has taken them to a foster home.

They lived in an old house with a bunch of other people, the address is 4774 W. Pacific Coast Highway in Lomita.

The way they got here is a little bit round about. A Welfare worker by the name of Sally Owens was doing a check on one of her cases when she saw this little girl, next door in the back yard. She was staggering around trying to keep up with her brother and sister. She looked so terrible that Ms. Owens asked her client about it and she wasn't forthcoming with any information, except that the kids were home alone during the day. Owens did a door knock, but nobody answered so she dialed us and I got the call.

I banged on the door and then went into the backyard when no one responded. Apparently, the kids were hiding so the place looked deserted. Based on what Ms. Owens had said about the poor condition of the one girl and the fact that there were two other small children possibly in need of emergency care, I pounded on the back door some more and when nobody answered, I forced entry. I found the kids in a back bedroom; the shades were down and it was obvious that they were trying to be invisible. Ms. Owens took one look at them, she knew that nobody was in charge, so she loaded them into her car and brought her here and then she took the others to a foster home.

One of our detectives has been in the neighborhood trying to get the status of the mom and dad. They work during the daytime and the neighbors think that the nine-year-old was sort of a substitute mother for the two little ones while the parents were away. One of the neighbors thinks that the school checked up on why the nine-year-old wasn't in school and the parents told them that she was sick and needed a lot of medical attention.

There are a lot of other people who come and go from the house, it looks like it's maybe a flop house for folks from south of the border who are here illegally. That's probably the case, I saw at least ten mattresses on the floor and a bunch of duffle bags and suitcases alongside of them.

I can't think of anything else to tell you, but if you think of anything, I'm working a double today so I'll be in the area until late this evening. OK ma'am?" Knox asked.

"Let me ask one more thing before you go, said Judy, does this little girl speak English?"

"She does but she's not going to become one of our dispatchers anytime soon, she's got a pretty strong accent and she slurs a lot of her words. The Docs think that she may slur because of the poisoning," he replied.

"OK, thanks for the information, and if I think of anything else, I'll give you a call. Be careful and thanks again."

"You're welcome ma'am," Knox said, as he packed up his reports and walked out the door.

Judy located the nursing supervisor in the Pediatric Intensive Care Unit, Susan Callaway. She was a middle-aged, motherly R.N. who looked like she belonged in a facility that dealt with sick kids. Judy got the rundown from her about Esther. It confirmed pretty much what Deputy Knox had told her in his shorthand synopsis. The little girl was gravely ill and so far, none of the diagnostics pointed to a specific disease.

One of the Docs who had examined Esther had a good deal of experience in Toxicology and was of the opinion that there was a very good chance that she had ingested some poisonous substance.

Nurse Callaway had spent some time at the bedside, trying to reassure the little girl that all they were trying to do was help her and that they wanted her to get well. During the conversation, Callaway had asked her if she had been sick for a long time and the response had been on the order of several weeks. She asked Esther if she was taking any medications and she had told her that the only thing she was taking was the medicine that mama or poppa gave her with a spoon and that it didn't taste good.

Judy asked the nurse if she might see and talk to the little girl and in a few moments, she found herself next to Esther's bed. She was hooked up to a cardiac monitor and she had several intravenous bottles dangling over her head and an oxygen rig plugged into her small nose.

In spite of her blue-gray color, she was a pretty little child and as she lay there, Judy felt a wave of pity and sorrow sweep through her. Helping the little girl deal with the strangers and the strangeness of the hospital was the doll that she had brought with her; it was a small, green, toy, plastic soldier. Esther was holding it to her chest and humming a quiet song, periodically she would stroke the soldier's head with her fingers and raise it to her bluish lips and give it a kiss. The soldier was obviously her dolly.

"Hello Esther," said Judy, "I'm here to try to find out why you needed to come to the hospital. The nurses and doctors say you are sick but right now they're not sure why. How do you feel?"

"My stomach hurts a lot and sometimes it's hard to see things and I get dizzy."

"Do you take anything for the sickness?" Judy asked.

"Momma and poppa give me medicine." Esther replied.

"Is it pills from the store?"

"No, it's from the bottle," said the little girl.

"Is it like a medicine from the drugstore?" Judy inquired.

"It's in the bottle in the kitchen cupboard by the sink; It's up high where the little ones won't get it."

Judy made small talk with Esther for several minutes and as she gently caressed the little girl's arm she watched as Esther did the same thing to her toy soldier.

"Do you have a soft, cuddly doll?" Wendy asked.

"Not any more, someone took it; poppa says it was a man who moved away. I wish he'd bring it back, it was my favorite doll."

"Can you tell me about her?"

Esther began describing her missing doll and it soon became apparent that it was a garden variety, department store doll with a soft body and limbs and a rubber or plastic head with eyes that blinked. The doll had been dressed in a white dress and black shoes.

"She sounds like a very nice dolly," said Judy as she rose to leave. "It was nice to talk to you Esther, I've got to go now, but I'll stop in and see you again. Bye now."

She had some things to do immediately and she soon found herself in back in the police waiting room and on the telephone. Judy's first call was to her unit, giving John Autrey a short overview of the case. She asked him to let their Sergeant know about it so that he'd know that it might end up being a fatal incident. Her second call was to Lomita Station where she talked to Sergeant Tony Sully about the possibility of getting some help. What she needed to do was a surveillance of the house on Pacific Coast Highway.

"I need somebody who can speak Spanish to give me a hand," she said as she explained her plan that was to wait until one of the occupants returned to the house. She and her partner would approach that individual and through a little "official pressure," which would involve talking about the Border Patrol and Immigration, they would gain permission to search for and obtain the bottle of "medicine". They would pour off a sample of the contents and send it to the hospital for analysis. The rest they'd book as evidence.

They'd try to get a statement from that individual about the circumstances of Esther's illness and they'd be inside waiting for Momma and Poppa Sanchez. Those two would be going directly to jail for child endangerment. Once at Lomita Station they could separate the two of them and attempt to interrogate them about the cause of their daughter's illness as well as the neglect of the kids.

Sully was enthusiastic in his response. "I'll get you help, the best and the most experienced, a dogged interrogator, an investigator who causes grown men to quake, an excellent bilingual bonus recipient and the person with the keys to our surveillance van, a perfect partner for you."

"That's wonderful," said Judy, "who is this gem?"

"Me… where do you want to meet up?"

Judy gave him the house address and he supplied the coordinates for the closest coffee shop where they'd leave her car. Then they'd go sit on the house, peering through the one-way glass of the surveillance van, until there was some activity.

The last call Judy made was to Lennox Sheriff's Station where she was connected to Lieutenant Nipps, the day

Watch Commander. She explained her predicament with the arrival of her husband's plane at L.A. Airport, a few miles from Lennox Station and the conflict with the ongoing investigation. "Can you have someone meet him and either drive him home or take him to my car? It's in Lomita's area.

"Tell ya what Judy, if you'll swear to your husband's reliability, we just might lend him one of our unmarked units and then both of you will have wheels under you. How does that sound?" said Nipps.

"It sounds fine, thanks for helping me out, I really appreciate it and I'm sure Rick will too. He's coming in at 16:22 hrs. on United flight 743."

"It's always a pleasure to help out our boss and his lady, especially a few days before he's due here to conduct an inspection. Besides, Duane is a genuinely good boss and anybody here would give him a hand," Nipps said.

"Charlie, you never are at a loss for an opportunity to suck up to the big guys," commented Judy, "seriously, thank you again !!"

It was still raining when Judy left the hospital, she traveled west along Pacific Coast Highway until she saw Roberts Coffee Shop and pulled into their half full lot. The lunch hour had passed and there were plenty of empty parking spaces. As she unfurled her umbrella and got out of her car, she saw Tony Sully come from the far side of an older Dodge van that resembled something the phone company might utilize. It was white with a blue stripe around it, below the windows, and several ladders were mounted on the roof. Judy knew that she'd be spending the next hour or several inside that van.

"Hi Tony, thanks for the help, it's nice of you to drop things and come out here to sit in the rain with me. I hope this isn't interfering with anything too important." Said Judy.

"I've got cabin fever Judy, it seems like I've been locked up in the station for over a week."

"With the rain and vacations, I just haven't been out, I'm glad you called, it's given me an excuse to get away and do some police work for a little while. Tell me what you want me to help with and I'll do it," Tony said.

"I'd like to set up close to the house, so that if someone shows up, we can be on them before they're in the door. Then it's pretty much like I told you over the phone, we nab whoever that is, get a permissive search and get the so called "medicine" bottle that's in the cupboard by the sink. If we can get any info from this person about what's in the bottle or what's going on with the little girl that's even better. I'd like to hear how long these kids have been left alone, so if your Spanish is fluent enough to find out the answers to these questions it would be a big help," said Judy.

"No problemo, senora." Said Tony. "I'll park this rig just west of the house, that way we can eyeball the sidewalk, driveway and front door. When we see a target make an approach, we'll bail out the side van door and be on him in a flash. I'll do a fast verbal routine and get us invited in. Once we're inside we should probably sit tight until the kid's folks make the scene. Them, we can finesse outside and once we're near the van we can arrest them, hook them up and have them at the station in no time."

"Sounds OK to me," said Judy.

"Well then let's do it," said Tony. "You should probably get in the back of the van while we're here so you won't have to crawl around once we're set down. And before I forget, I ran the location through our event index and we've not had a call that amounts to anything at that house or on that block for over sixteen months, so we're not going to be in the middle of anything that we know of."

Tony pulled a couple of magnetic signs from atop the engine cover inside the van and affixed them to the front doors and then stood back to admire his work. "Tony's Quality Appliance Repair," they read and indicated a telephone number that was connected to an answering machine in the station Detective Bureau. He produced a windbreaker and slipped into it and Judy saw it was embroidered with the same words on the van. "Will we blend in or what?" Tony inquired.

A few minutes later the two of them were seated in the rear of the van that had an interior specially designed for doing surveillance. There was a bank of radios and cell phones all equipped with optional headsets so that noise from within had little likelihood of escaping from the well-insulated interior. There were a variety of cameras, both still and video and low light. There were directional microphones, raid jackets, ballistic vests and a collection of entry tools and weapons. The van had an almost silent air conditioning system, refrigerator and a chemical toilet with a privacy shroud.

"This is a nice unit," said Judy, "did you pick it up as a cast off from one of the Headquarters units?"

"No," replied Tony. "We had a rash of residential burglaries a couple years ago up in the Rancho Palos Verdes area and some of the local citizens learned that our station surveillance rig was a do it yourself kit version. Anyway, after we caught the burglars they volunteered to buy and build us what we would like, and this is it."

Tony spotted a small statured, Latino male coming up behind them. He was soaking wet and had been out in the weather for some time." Get ready to go; I think our first target is in sight."

Judy was surprised how quick and agile Tony was. He was out of the van and had collared the man as he had stepped from the sidewalk toward the house. Judy stood close and listened to the rapid-fire Spanish conversation between the two men. After several minutes Tony turned to her and explained that the fellow, he was talking to did in fact live in the house. He had invited them to come in with him and to search for the bottle of "medicine," which they found immediately.

"This guy has only been here a little over a week, he's still trying to find work and in this weather nobody's hiring day laborers, but he's so low on funds he's willing to stand outside near the hardware store on the off chance somebody may hire him. He says that there are only three kids living here and his descriptions match up with the three that came out of here earlier. The oldest seems to be the chief cook and bottle washer for the other two, even though she's sick, she has the responsibility for the others.

Both of the folks have jobs, he thinks they work in some big restaurant over in San Pedro. They've never told him what's the matter with the sick kid but he's seen them give her some of the "medicine" and that usually happens right after they get home. They are usually the first adults to arrive home after work since they have a car.

I think this guy's being straight with me, I told him we don't work immigration cases but if I thought he was lying to me- that before the sun rises tomorrow, he'd be looking at a bus ride south, courtesy of INS. If he's truthful we'll leave him alone. I also told him that sometimes cops up here pay for help and information; this twenty in my shirt pocket is for him if and when we leave with the two you want."

"Thanks Tony, I'm glad I took you up on your help offer, you do a great job and all I have to do is stand back and watch you work. This day started ugly but it looks like it's going to end OK. I guess our next effort is just hanging around and waiting for my two to show up," said Wendy. "How about we turn the T.V. on and take turns watching the news or the driveway for our next guests

When we see them arrive, we'll wait here for them to come in and then you can be Mr. Smooth and tell them that we're cops on a mission of mercy and need them to come with us to get their kids. Once they're outside we'll hook them up, the guy first and then his wife. How's that sound?"

"Is this the way the big city cops do it?" Tony asked. "It's fine with me, our first visitor says nobody here has any weapons as far as he knows. He did say that the next two are not real enthused about doing anything that might get them sent back home to live in the same hut as the chickens and goats. So, I suspect it will go alright until they know they're going to go to jail, then they might bolt."

Judy replied with a suggestion. "Why don't we get a black and white to hang around out on the Highway, when our guests arrive, we let them know via radio and they roll in and back us up?"

"That makes sense," Tony said as he keyed his small, handheld radio and switched to the station tactical frequency.

In a short time, Tony had communicated with the area patrol cars and had arranged for them to respond to the house when requested. Two one-man units were available and would stand by in the vicinity pending the request to respond.

At 5:15 PM Judy saw a dilapidated Toyota pull into the driveway and two figures began walking swiftly toward the door, trying to avoid as many raindrops as possible. Tony was on the radio advising the patrol units to initiate their response and to stand by outside until they saw a procession of people approaching the van.

It worked perfectly, Tony schmoozed the couple right out the door and was still holding their attention when the uniformed Deputies approached and assisted in the arrest. The rain had produced little in the way of police activity in the area and when the uniformed guys offered to transport the two arrestees to the station both Judy and Tony were happy to accept.

The two Detectives re-entered the house and Judy looked around for a soft doll or toy that she might take to Esther on her next visit to the hospital, but she wasn't successful in locating anything that a sick little girl could cuddle up with in her hospital bed.

Tony found the first resident waiting apprehensively but after he gave him the twenty-dollar bill the guy acted so happy it was hard not to smile along with him. He followed them to the door and waved good-bye.

After they arrived at the Station, Judy got her prisoners booked at the station and arranged for Immigration holds after determining their illegal status in the United States, thanks to Tony's bilingual skills. She then transferred a sample of the "medicine" into a vial and took it to the hospital for their analysis in determining whether it had anything to do with Esther's condition.

She decided that she'd wait until tomorrow to interrogate her prisoners, thinking that a night in jail might be of some psychological assistance. She confirmed that Esther's brother and sister were safely placed in temporary foster homes. She called her office and let them know she was going off duty and then she went home to Duane.

It was almost 8 PM when she walked through the door. Duane was there, eating a recently delivered pizza and drinking a glass of Chianti. He rose from his make shift dining area on the family room couch in front of the T.V. when she came into the room and they hugged and kissed one another hello. They were glad to see each other and their smiles seemed to light up the room.

She joined him for a couple of slices of pizza and a glass of wine and then asked him to go with her to the local department store for a crash shopping visit.

"Now!! Can't it wait until tomorrow?" He asked.

"Not really," she said, It's OK I'll go alone, you've been traveling all day and I'll be back in less than an hour. I should have done it on the way home but I wanted to see you first. Give me a kiss and promise not to leave until I get back, OK, big boy?

"Oh, alright, I'll come along but it had better be important." Said Duane.

The drive to the store was only five minutes and, in that time, Judy had tried to tell Duane about Esther, the little blue-gray girl who lay dying in a hospital with only a toy soldier to soften her suffering. Judy found that her voice got a little mushy as she talked and she wasn't surprised to find tears welling in her eyes. "The Docs think she's been poisoned and I think her parents did it to her but I don't know why."

"This one's got to you, hasn't it honey?" Duane asked, and he put his arm around her shoulder, reaching across the Jeep Cherokee to touch her. "Is that why we're going shopping, to get that poor little kid a doll?"

Judy found that she couldn't say yes. All that could come out of her was a soft, "uh huh" and she found that the lights outside their car had taken on an added glistening from the tears that were now rolling down her cheeks.

"I love you honey," Duane said. "But if I go into that store with a cute lady who is crying and end up buying her a dolly, the sales staff will have a story to tell for months."

"I'll be OK, I didn't know this was bothering me until right now," said Judy. "Can you imagine being nine years old and being the little mother to two littler kids, all day? Not being able to go to school or play with kids your own age or have any toys, not even a real doll?"

Duane parked their car in the store lot, as close as he could to the entrance. Then the two of them dashed through the rain into the department store and quickly found the toy section and the dolls. Judy found the one that she thought might make Esther happy. It was a soft body doll with a rubber head and eyes that blinked; it was dressed in a white frilly dress and white shoes. Judy hoped that Esther wouldn't mind the color of the shoes but there weren't any white dressed dolls with black shoes.

As they got back into the Jeep for the return ride home Judy touched Duane's cheek and whispered in a Mae West-like voice: "I'd like to snuggle up in bed with you, a glass of wine and a fire in our fireplace. With the rain beating on our roof, I'll bet I could be convinced to get incredibly romantic with the man I love."

"Keep an eye out for cops dear, this old Cherokee's about to fly!!" Duane yelled.

In spite of the bravado, Duane got them home safely. They were soon in bed and, as a small fire burned softly behind the glass doors of their bedroom fireplace, they snuggled up and fell asleep in each other's arms.

"That was incredibly romantic snoring last night, my dear." Duane said, as he emerged from the bathroom with his battery-powered shaver in his hand. "I don't know who fell asleep first, but when I woke up the fire was out, my arm was asleep and someone was running a chain saw in my ear and I'm pretty sure it was you."

"What can I say, I had the wickedest of intentions but my cheering section ran out of gas too. We must have been exhausted, I didn't wake up at all until just now." Said Judy.

Would you come with me to the hospital this morning? I want to drop off the doll to the little girl and while I'm there I can check and see if the hospital lab found anything of interest in the vial, I brought for them,"

"Duane looked at her and said, "you know I don't like those places, they're filled with sick people and it always reminds me of my own mortality. Why do you want me to go?"

"You were sweet enough to go with me to get the doll last night and I'd just like you to be there when I give it to her, I think she'll be happy to get it and besides it's good for a grown man to see a little kid smile. Won't you please come? I promise it will only take a few minutes and you won't have to stay. Please Honey?" Judy asked.

After they had showered, dressed and eaten a quick breakfast, they headed to the hospital in separate cars and met outside the Emergency Ward entrance. Judy led Duane through the maze of corridors to the Pediatric Intensive Care Unit and introduced him to Susan Callaway.

The nurse looked at the doll Judy carried and said, "you're a sweetheart," I've watched that little girl with that toy soldier too. It didn't dawn on me to bring her a doll but I'm sure glad you did. She's awake now and it would be a good time to give it to her, before the day starts with its battery of tests and procedures for her."

Before entering the room, Judy handed the doll to Duane and asked him to hide it behind his back.

"Hi Esther, remember me from yesterday? Well, I am back and I want you to meet my husband Duane. We've got something that we hope you will like," Judy said as she nodded at Duane. "Can you guess what it is?"

Esther looked at the two of them through her red rimmed eyes and asked very quietly, "you brought something for me? I don't know what it is."

Judy went to the edge of the little girl's bed and Duane slowly moved the doll into Esther's view and as he did a smile came to the little blue-gray lips and it grew by inches the closer the doll came toward her.

"You brought me a dolly?" Esther said incredulously, "my own dolly." Then she reached out and took it in her small hands and looked at it for a moment. "She's so pretty, I love her. Can I really have her?"

"She's really yours," said Judy. Duane, who was strangely silent, said nothing. Instead he moved his hand to the little girl's cheek and touched it softly.

"I'll take care of her, Esther said, it will be so nice to have a real dolly again." She looked at Duane and asked, "you were nice to get me the dolly, will you help me give her a name?"

"You could call her Judy," Rick said.

"That's a nice name, I like it. That is what I will call her," the little girl replied. "I don't have anything to give you except this," she said to Duane as she handed him the small green plastic, toy soldier.

His large hand closed around the little toy and he could only say one word, "Thanks." Then he turned and walked out of the room and stood silently at the nurse's station looking around and into the other rooms where other sick and dying little children lay.

Judy joined him after a few minutes. "She likes her doll and she likes you," she said.

"What happens to these kids?" Duane asked Susan Callaway.

"Unfortunately, by the time we get them, the majority of them are terminally ill. Hardly any of them ever go home from here and that's the tragic reality. Some of our patients are comatose, most are so weak that they're bed ridden, our job is to try and make them comfortable and to help those who love them come to grips with the sad reality," replied Susan.

"It must take a very special kind of person to work here." Said Duane.

"Yes, it does, everyone in the unit goes through specialized training in how to handle death and dying, particularly small children. No one is assigned here against their will, everyone is a volunteer. We all pull together to help the children, their families and each other. I'm the senior nurse in the unit, I've been here almost ten years," said Susan.

"In my opinion you and those who work here with you deserve the equivalent of Medicines Medal of Valor," said Duane. "Can I ask if the kids who are conscious ever have visitors?"

"Certainly, their friends and families are permitted to see them and we encourage them to come here often, as long as they don't interrupt the hospital routine or the other patients, they are welcome." Susan replied.

Duane left the hospital and Judy remained for a while to see if the hospital lab had run an analysis on the vial, she'd left for them. The lab technician she was looking for was in a staff consultation and wouldn't be available until later in the day. Judy left about twenty minutes after Duane and went to Lomita Station to sit in on the interrogation of her two prisoners.

She met Tony Sully in the Station coffee room and after pouring a cup she sat across the table from him and asked if he were sure he would be available to help her again today. "I can get a Spanish speaker from my unit if you're tied up on something else," she offered.

"No way Judy, I'm enjoying this. It's a little out of the ordinary from our garden variety burglaries, car thefts and muggings and I'm interested in helping you find out if these people poisoned the little kid," said Tony.

"They brought the prisoners out individually, from their separate cells in the Station jail and escorted them to the windowless, 10-foot square interrogation room, near the Detective Bureau offices. They had agreed to begin with Maria Sanchez, the twenty-eight-year-old mother of the three children.

She was a nervous woman who sat, fidgeting, across the table from the two detectives. Tony turned on a small tape recorder and began, speaking in Spanish, advising Maria of her Miranda rights. After hearing them and agreeing to waive them and talk with the Detectives, she signed her name to a form indicating the process and voluntary waiver.

She began responding to Judy's questions through Tony. She told them that they had come to this country illegally five years ago and when they first arrived, she worked at home, sewing piecework and watching Esther and her baby brother, Hector. She did that until a little over a year after the birth of their youngest child. Then they decided they needed a larger income and that is when she went to work with her husband, Miguel in the restaurant.

She soon admitted to knowingly leaving her two small children in the care of her oldest daughter, nine-year-old Esther. Her reasoning was simple; if they hired a baby sitter or put the kids in childcare, they would not have money to send back to Guatemala, to their families who were desperately poor.

In her homeland, what they did was not unusual. Esther had been to school; she could speak and write English and Spanish and could do mathematics. What else did a child need to know? She was a responsible girl and was very capable of being the little mother to the young ones.

Judy shifted gears quickly on Maria. "Tony, tell her we've talked to her husband and that he's told us that she was the one to give Esther the stuff that made her sick and that it was all her idea. We want to know why she'd do that?"

Tony translated and they watched as Maria turned pale and then she nervously spoke and told them that her husband was not telling the truth. When they were enroute to the United States, the man they'd paid the money to bring them here had told them that if a family was here illegally, they would not be deported if they had a child who was sick and required medical care.

When the School officials had inquired about Esther, they had lied and told them that the little girl was sick and needed medical attention. They thought that they had been found out and were soon to be deported. It was her husband's idea to make Esther ill enough so that they could stay in this country and he was the one who would make the "medicine."

Maria was shaken when they told her that the little girl was in the hospital and was very sick. She broke down and laid her head on the interrogation room table and began sobbing. Tony shut the tape recorder off and turned to Wendy and asked, "got enough from her?"

"I'd like to know what they put in the "medicine", said Wendy.

Tony turned the recorder on again and managed to get Maria coherent enough to answer the questions he poised to her. She explained that she didn't know everything that went into the bottle however, Karo syrup to which was added things including perfume, antifreeze, shellac, shoe polish, and metal polish. They'd dose her, generally every day, with a big spoonful of the concoction.

"Let's take a break and then we'll get it on with poppa," suggested Judy.

"I like your idea, I'll race you to the coffee room," Tony challenged.

"No way," said Judy, "I saw you move last night when you exploded out of the van, I know when I'm outmatched. I'll even buy coffee.

Their conversation was interrupted by a telephone page for Judy. She picked up a phone in the Detective Bureau and the station phone operator made the connection. "Hi Judy, this is John Autrey, we just got a call from Nurse Callaway at Harbor General Hospital, your little victim just passed away. It's now Homicide Bureau's case and they're asking you to standby at Lomita Station with your suspects. They'll be along shortly to interview or re-interview them."

Judy was silent for a moment and the silence was interrupted by Autrey's inquiry about whether she was still there.

"Yes, John, I heard what you said, I just didn't think it would be so sudden, I just spoke to the little girl this morning and she was happy when we left. I guess I've just had the wind knocked out of me, but I'll be OK," said Judy.

"Tony, if you don't mind, I'm going to skip the coffee, I'm going to walk a couple of laps around the Station parking lot instead."

"Are you all right," asked Tony, concerned about Judy's sudden change.

"Ya, I'm OK, my nine-year-old victim has died and I just need to be alone for a little while. I hope you'll understand." Judy replied.

"I sure do, look, I'll be at my desk if you need anything just let me know and it's yours." Tony responded.

The rest of the morning involved a turn-over of the information Judy had gathered to a couple of Homicide Detectives so that they could pursue a murder case against Esther's momma and poppa. By noon she was so troubled by the death of the little girl that she found herself back in the parking lot at Harbor General Hospital. She had been thinking to herself that she'd gotten too close to this victim. In spite of her thoughts, she walked into the Pediatric Intensive Care Unit, looking for Susan Callaway.

The matronly nurse saw Judy first and came to her and gave her a hug and as she did, she whispered to her, "don't go blaming yourself, you did the very best you could to help that sweet little girl. It wasn't you who put her here, you only tried to help her and God will bless you for that. The first few hours are the worst, trust me honey, it will get better. You should know that she went gently, when the nurse answered her alarm she was already gone, hugging the doll that you were nice enough to give to her."

Somehow, she got through the rest of the day and managed to get home before Duane did. She was in the process of making dinner when he arrived. After he walked in the door and kissed her hello, he told her that the morning hospital visit had been on his mind all day.

"What would you think the hospital would say if I asked them to permit the Sheriff's Department to adopt that Sick Kid Unit?" He asked.

"Adopt, what do you mean?"

"Well, periodically uniformed and civilian members of the Department could visit those little kids who can tolerate visitors, we'd talk to them, hug them, give them a toy and maybe some token from the Department. We'd try to bring those little kids a couple minutes of happiness. You know as well as I do that little kids usually like cops, maybe we could make them smile.

I think it would be nice for the kids and it could be meaningful to the Deputies and our Civilian employees as well. It can put them in touch with a good side of their community. I just think it would be a positive experience for everyone. If what happened to me this morning is any indicator, I'd be willing to try it in a heartbeat." Duane said.

"You can call Susan Callaway tomorrow and ask her what she thinks about the idea. I'm pretty sure if she likes it, it will be a go, and she's the nurse in charge and has been there, as you heard, longer than anybody." Wendy said.

"They finished dinner and were relaxing in the family room after the dishes were done.

Duane had put a compact disc on the stereo and they were listening to the Three Tenors when Judy sat down next to Duane on their leather sofa. "I've got something to tell you, that may spoil your evening or your adoption idea," she said.

"Well, let me have it," Duane said.

"Esther passed away today," I talked to Susan Callaway and she said that she "fell asleep and never woke up." The Life Support alarm went off and they called a Code Blue but they weren't able to resuscitate her. Susan says she has gone to a better place where little kids can run and play to their heart's content and people won't poison them, Judy said as she put her arms around Duane. "I didn't want to tell you when you walked in the door, I decided it would be better to wait until now."

Duane sat there silent for several minutes, bent forward with his elbows on his knees and his chin cradled in his hands. He sat upright slowly and reached into his right front pants pocket and withdrew a small, green plastic toy soldier. "I don't know why but I've been carrying this around with me all day."

"I know why, it's because you're a good man and you care about people, in spite of that sometimes, Mr. Tough Guy, role you put on. That why I love you so much." Judy said, as she nuzzled her lips into the back of his neck.

The next day Duane made his call to Susan Callaway and she surprised him with the enthusiasm of her response. These are invisible kids, they're so far gone that they're not candidates for a trip to Disneyland or a ride on a fire truck. To have cops come in here and make them feel special is a wonderful idea. You've got my support and I'll talk to my administrators into giving this a thumbs up and I'll get back to you as soon as I hear.

Duane heard that afternoon that Susan had gotten a "Go" from the hospital brass and as they talked, they planned the first event together. It would be several weeks away.

The planning and preparation took an hour or two hours out of Duane's days in the ensuing weeks, and finally the day arrived.

Duane kept a diary, and the evening following the event he wrote this entry.

"The pain was in her eyes and it was not fully dulled by whatever was in the tube that hung from the chrome and glass hospital I-V rig that ran into her slender arm."

"She rested quietly in her hospital bed, her seven-year old chest breathing quickly; she was a very sick girl. She was in the same room that a few weeks ago I had visited with Judy and where I had met Esther."

"There was a soft knocking on the door frame of her hospital room and her head shifted slowly as she moved to see what new poking, probing or testing might now befall her."

"Looming in the doorway was a seven-foot tall, electric pink, blue eyed rabbit. "Hello Sweetheart," said the rabbit. Her head twisted a little more and now a quizzical expression crept to her face."

"Buenos Dias, mija," intoned a red-nosed clown who joined the rabbit in the door."

"A small, Mona Lisa smile came and went fleetingly. The rabbit, the clown, now Superman and some uniformed Deputy Sheriff's entered the room."

"All of them were members of the Los Angeles County Sheriff's Department. They encircled her bed, smiled and touched her hand and her face and they gave her a small plush puppy. She held it tightly. As they began to leave, waving as they left, she waved back. I watched her once she was again alone, she let out a big sigh and hugged the puppy a little tighter and the fleeting smile appeared again."

"On they went, to the next room to work another second or two of magic. I looked up and down the halls for television cameras, for someone who might complain about the misuse of resources or criticize their actions.

They weren't there and I was glad. Some moments of being a cop are just too special to share."

"The Deputies, civilian employees, all volunteers, did what they did on their own time and Duane was very proud of them."

He was also glad to carry around, where nobody has to see it, a little green plastic soldier that he got from a very special little mother a while ago."

"How did it go, dear?" Judy asked that evening, inquiring about the visit to the hospital."

"Better than I ever imagined," said Duane as he stood in the kitchen doorway, talking as Judy cooked their dinner. He looked fondly at a small green soldier that lay on the kitchen counter, next to his car keys. "God keep you well, Esther," he prayed silently. Then he began to recount the day.

LIST OF CONTRIBUTORS: ...

Jack Boberg
Chuck & Corky Jackson
Larry Brademeyer
Dan Burt
Ken Cable
George Collins
Jerry Conklin
Bob Edmonds
Dick Foreman
Carole Freeman
Dave Hagthrop
Larry Jenks
Pat Massey
Tom McNeil
Moon Mullen
Joe Oblek
Steve Pair
Duane Preimsberger
Ken Ryall
Jimmy Smith
John Spiller
Ed Young

MORNING WATCH FOLLY'S

by Duane Preimsberger, Assist Sheriff, retired

Charlie Knapp was a longtime vice detective; he'd worked bookmaking and then switched to morals for the last several years of his career. He was so good at his job and could invent so many characters that he was often able to arrest the same prostitute a half-dozen times or more. The girls were often embarrassed to realize that they'd been "tricked" by the same guy several times!

In the early morning hours while looking for a "date," he could become a genuine appearing Mississippi National Guard Colonel with an accent that went along with grits and gravy. He adapted a metal leg brace to his disguise and become a disabled guy limping convincingly along. Sometimes he'd stutter and his eyes would roll back as he negotiated price and services. With his dark, severely cut black suit and Germanic accent, Charlie became an embassy employee out for a good time. Since most of his efforts occurred I the early morning hours, he also could feign falling asleep while discussing details with the girls, pretending that he has Narcolepsy. Whatever he portrayed he did it convincingly and the girls came to see him as an adversary who was both talented and fair!

Charlie played by the rules; he made his arrests professionally and most often gently. He was demeaning or insulting and on occasion if the circumstances warranted, he wasn't beyond calling some hookers babysitter to tell that person that a particular girl would be home late. He even alerted bondsmen to the unlikelihood of a skip by one of his arrestees. The girls knew he was a cop and although they didn't necessarily like what he did on the job, they liked him as a human being! A few days before his last watch some of the girls along Sunset and Santa Monica Blvd. learned that Charlie was retiring and decided to throw him a surprise party on his last day. They alerted Vice Bureau brass and convinced a local motel owner that he should donate a bunch of room for the event. After looking economic disaster in the face, he quickly agreed. Several of the girls took the night off and spent hours decorating the rooms with fancy streamers and balloons made from the prophylactic tools of their trade. Others bought cake, punch, beer and other items including a huge birthday card that was signed by all the girls under the phrase, "From Your Tricks on The Boulevard!" Most of the Morals Crew attended as well as some Vice brass, A few special folks from West Hollywood Sheriff's Station and a couple dozen area girls showed up. The party was a great success. The attendees sang "Happy Retirement," and regaled the guests and Charlie with funny stories of their arrests by him and then they hugged him goodbye. It was an unusual gathering of cops and hookers gathered together to wish a fond farewell to an unusual guy who'd made his living putting some of the folks who were saluting him in jail. It was another story about life on the Morning Watch policing the streets in the jurisdiction of the Los Angeles County Sheriff's Department.

THE CRIPPLED GUY

BY Duane Preimsberger, Assist Sheriff, retired

I first got to meet the Crippled Guy in the summer of 1952, when I was 12 years old, although I'd known of him long before that. Like most boys, my friends and I were well acquainted with everybody in our neighborhood and we paid special attention to anyone who was different- like the "Crip."

He was a nice enough guy; he smiled a lot and always said, "Hi kid," to us as he rolled by in his wheelchair. The rumor was that he'd been injured in the war in the South Pacific and had lost the use of his legs after being hit by machine gun fire in a place called Guadalcanal. He looked perfectly normal from the waist up, but his legs, which were usually covered up on all but the hottest days by a plaid blanket, were withered and useless. Because of his injuries we called him the Crippled Guy or Crip for short.

He lived all by himself in a little house surrounded by an eye level hedge and with the exception of his shopping trips to the local stores; he wasn't often seen. When he was out, was a time of curiosity for the other kids and me. We'd watch him navigate as he rolled his chair down driveways and through alleys and parking lots trying to avoid difficult obstacles like narrow passages, curbs and stairs. During his trips he never asked for or took help from anyone. Occasionally, we'd see visitors go into his place and sometimes he'd leave with them in their car, driving away with his chair folded up and sticking out of the car trunk. He'd be gone for a while but he was never away for very long.

I managed to get a newspaper route that summer, delivering a throwaway that was published twice a week. My route covered about 100 nearby homes including the Crips. I rode my route, balancing acrobatically on my black, chrome fendered, Roadmaster bike, throwing papers onto front lawns from the carrier bags suspended from my handlebars. The Crips house posed a challenge for me with the hedge all around it. I couldn't see where the paper would land and I was fearful that if I threw it and broke something, I'd quickly become an unemployed paperboy.

I sat on my bike in front of the Crip's house trying to figure out what to do and finally, I took a deep breath, got off my bike and approached his solid wooden front gate. There was a little tin sign nailed to it that read, "No Trespassers!"

"I hope that's not me," I thought as I pressed the doorbell on the gate frame. A few minutes later, I heard the sound of rolling wheels crunching on gravel and then the Crip opened the gate.

For a few seconds he just sat there looking at me curiously from his chair and then a friendly smile appeared on his face as he asked, "what do ya want, kid?" As I explained my dilemma the smile got bigger and when I was done, he replied; "just drop the paper over the gate kid, and thanks for asking, I've got some stuff that could be hurt if it got bombed by a newspaper. By the way, have you ever seen a Koi?"

"A what?" I asked

"A Koi."

"What's a Koi?"

"A fish, wanna see some?'

"I guess so."

The Crip reversed his chair effortlessly and told me to follow him and as I did, I entered a world I didn't know existed in my neighborhood. Even to my young mind, I knew I was entering a special place. I know now, it was a Japanese garden; complete with carefully manicured Banzai plantings, stone lanterns, patterns of stepping stones sand, gravel and a small wooden bridge over the center of a figure eight shaped pond. In the pond were a dozen or more of the biggest gold fish my twelve- year old eyes had ever seen. "Those are Koi," the Crip said, motioning at the fish that swam below as we watched them from the bridge.

"Watch this," he said as he took a small tidbit from a bag that was hooked to the side of his chair. He bent forward, toward the water and his hand nearly touched the surface of the pond. Immediately, the big fish moved toward him and several of them literally propelled themselves partially out of the water, taking the food from his hand. "Wanna feed em?" he inquired, offering me the bag.

In a heartbeat, I was leaning off the bridge holding a tidbit in my fingers

Inches above the water while big lipped fish nibbled at the treat, I offered them. It was the beginning of a friendship between me and the fish and me and the Crip. As the summer progressed, I found more reasons to visit the fish as well as my new friend.

Part way through that summer season, he asked me if I'd be willing to work for him helping in the yard and gardens. "I'll pay 25 cents an hour, but your folks are going to have to tell me it's OK, so have them come and see me and we'll talk."

"Hey mom!! Will ya go over to the Crips and tell him it's OK with you if I work for him for 25 cents an hour?" This question initiated a long discussion about who the Crip was, where he lived, why I knew him, how much time had I been spending there, what was I doing and why hadn't I told her. After those questions and more were asked and answered to her satisfaction, there was only one addition.

"What's a Koi?"

In the end, mom agreed to meet the Crip and to discuss with him my pending employment. The two of them talked for a long time and when mom finally came home, I could hardly wait to ask my question about the suitability of the job for me and I was delighted to learn it was mine.

That evening after dinner, I heard my mom having one of those adult talks with my dad that kids aren't supposed to hear. "They moved here from Hawaii after learning that he was permanently paralyzed. She ran off with some low life creep and they took his son with them. He's never heard a thing about them since the day they left and her relatives refuse to give him any information. He really misses his son who is the same age as our boy."

I couldn't understand why anybody would run away from the Crippled Guy, he was a nice man. I wondered what his kid thought about not being with his dad anymore and if the low life was good to him.

I soon started to working in the Japanese garden and found out quickly that the job wasn't easy. The Crip didn't pull any punches, I worked! I had to be on time, pay attention, do what I was told, put the tools and equipment away and be respectful. On top of that my work got inspected and sometimes I had to do it over in order to get it right. I learned that the phrase, "I'm disappointed in your effort," was not a commendation for workman like behavior and by the end of the summer, I'd managed to avoid hearing it most off the time. Doing good work had tangible results, before long I was earning a couple of bucks extra a week. I could squander money on Hop a long Cassidy movie, comic books, yo-yos, candy bars, marbles and the really neat reward, a multiple bladed Swiss Army Knife. Life was great.

There was an unexpected benefit that came from working for the Crip. His house was filled with low bookshelves and hundreds of books and a few trinkets including one he wouldn't talk about. The mystery was a small shadowbox frame containing three items; silver captains collar insignia, a Silver Star and a Purple Heart.

However, he enjoyed talking about the books and as he spoke, he taught me stuff, mostly about his volumes and writers like Cervantes, Shakespeare, Kipling, Doyle, Hemingway, Steinbeck and others. He told me about their lives and he encouraged me to read their works. He loaned me his leather-bound volumes from the collections of many, many books in his house. When I brought them back, he'd quiz me about what I had read while I worked and as he sat in his wheelchair overseeing my efforts at maintenance gardening. He made sure I'd missed little in my reading.

One day I asked him to tell me the title of his favorite book and for the first time ever, he was slow to respond. He sat in his wheelchair and looked at the ground for a moment before he replied, "I guess it's got to be "Don Quixote."

"Can I read it?" I asked.

"Sure."

"What's it about?"

"It's really a political satire, but few people reading it now know that."

"Oh."

In the next few days, I became immersed in the book and I became a junior Don Quixote as I read about the Knight of the Woeful Countenance, his Squire Sancho and the Lady Dulcinea. The battles with windmills and the righting of wrongs fascinated and intrigued me. As I read the book and tried to prepare myself for the test that would come from the Crip, I was struck by the similarity that existed between the character in Cervantes work and the Crippled Guy who had become my friend, teacher and mentor. Both men had been struggling to deal with adversity and injustice to the best of their abilities.

I guess I grew up a little bit that summer, I began to understand how a terribly injured man could wrestle with all of the difficulties of his life on a daily basis and do it without losing his humanity or sense of humor or his appreciation for life and beauty.

That summer, Don Quixote became my favorite story as well and through the many years that have passed since my path crossed the one rolled by the Crippled Guy, I have cherished the tale. For me, it too has never been a political work, it is a story of a man who believes in what he's doing and tries to do the very best he can with what he's got.

In my home, in the family room, there is a worn, dog-eared, 1900's, leather bound copy of Cervantes book as well as several statues, made from papier Mache, wood, porcelain and metal; images of the Knight of the Woeful Countenance, Don Quixote de la Mancha. I suppose the book and statues are a quiet tribute to a Crippled Guy who touched the life of a 12- year old boy many years ago by demonstrating how to do the best he could with what he had. We stayed friends until he moved away. Bulldozers demolished his house and garden and replaced that very special place with a civic complex. When it was gone a little bit of magic disappeared from my life. Once he left the neighborhood, I never got to see him again and that has always saddened me. I learned later that the Crippled Guy died after several years in a Veteran Administration Hospital. Every now and again something I read or see reminds me of the Crip and as a matter of fact through the years I've been to see the play, "Man of La Mancha," at least a half dozen times. Whenever I read something about the story or the play, I invariably think of him. The Crip, I'm sure, hoped to give me an interest and an appreciation for books and classic writers as well as an appreciation for overcoming adversity. He did well in meeting his goals and objectives and as I look back, I'm sorry that I never had the opportunity to tell him thank you or see him after he moved away. He made a lifelong contribution to my being and I believe that I'm a better person for having had the opportunity to be touched by his determination, intelligence, kindness and his caring.

WALDO THE TALKING DUCK

by Duane T. Preimsberger, Assist. Sheriff, retired

Willowbrook is a four-square mile community sandwiched in between Watts to the north and Compton to the south. Although the name would suggest a bucolic and peaceful community it wasn't always so and I frequently wondered how the name came to be. Unfortunately, I was never able to find the brook although there were a few weeping willows in the neighborhood. In the late 1950's and early 1960's most of the area was residential housing that dated back to the 1920's. These small wooden framed dwellings were often on large lots ranging from a third of an acre to a full one and in the backyards were often chickens, ducks, rabbits, goats that augmented dinner tables. It wasn't unusual for the Los Angeles County Deputy Sheriff's from Firestone Sheriff's Station who patrolled the area to see these critters during their watch.

Deputy Richard Foreman and his partner were working the morning watch from 11:00 PM until 7:00 AM in Willowbrook when they came across their very first case of Willowbrook duck napping. It was almost 3:00 AM, a time when in almost every community the need for police services reaches the bottom of the chart. Most people are sleeping or at least at home, in bed. That why the partners were more than just a little surprised to see a man with a huge pot belly and two heads walking determinedly south along Willowbrook Ave. He was dressed in dark clothing and in the shadowy light he might have been invisible but his unusual appearance drew attention.

"Pull over, we've got to check this one out," commented Richard as their black and white patrol car pulled to the curb alongside the unusual man.

One of the heads turned toward the Deputies and began quacking as Richard and his partner quickly realized that there was a live duck underneath the light-weight jacket worn by the suspicious person. The duck's body was producing the giant belly and it had stuck its head up along the jacket collar, accounting for the second face that was next to the more normal human head.

"Good morning sir, we've stopped you because it's a little unusual to see a person walking the streets at this hour with a duck concealed under his jacket."

"What duck?"

At that point Richard, who possesses a remarkable quick wit and a keen sense of humor decided to play along while making up the script as he continued the conversation.

"Well sir, it appears to us that you have somehow obtained 'Waldo,' the famous talking duck who has been reported duck napped. When we came on duty, we were all briefed on the duck napping and we were advised to be on the lookout for a very dangerous and wanted suspect who had taken Waldo. I believe sir, that's you!"

"I didn't kidnap no duck," replied the crook. "What duck?" asked Richard.

"Y'all must mean the one I found walking down the street and decided to take home so's he could be warm that's why he be in my coat."

"Sir, your story is difficult to believe, my partner and I think that you came upon Waldo through nefarious and disingenuous means and have acquired him in an effort to recover the substantial reward offered for his safe re-unitement with his caretakers!" "Say What?"

Sir, you stole Waldo, thus committing the crime of aggravated duck napping."

"I didn't do none of them genius or necropious things. I was just walking along when the duck came right out in front of me on the sidewalk! All I wanted to do was to help him out." "Can you take us back to where you found him?" "Sure can."

A few minutes later the trio + duck were parked in front of a home on 118th St. and after just a brief conversation with the residents the Deputies determined that a duck was indeed missing from their duck enclosure and that the missing fowl bore an exact resemblance to the duck under the coat of the now profusely sweating suspect.

"Well there is no doubt about it now; you duck napped Waldo from the pen in the backyard here. He was here on a short vacation with family, getting away from the glamour and glitz of show business, just resting and relaxing and simply being a duck when you napped him. Holy Mackerel man, the Federal Government is going to put you away for years and years! Newspapers, radio and television are going to write you up big time for this Federal offense. You'll be old and gray by the time you get out."

"But I didn't duck .033332nap that duck, give me one of them Pollengraph tests and I'll pass it cause I ain't lyin' or denyin." "Sir, have you seen our new field polygraph unit that our patrol cars are fitted with?" "No, I ain't,"

Well it works on a modified electrical connectivity premise that measures redundant electrolysis impulses in your hand that is pressed against the cover of our spotlight. These impulses are then calibrated based upon your age, gender and the ambient outside temperature and that information is converted into a signal; "lie," or "no lie," that is projected to the lights on our Motorola radio. Green means no lie and red means lie. Would you be willing to submit to the test?" "Yes, I will!"

Soon, Richard had the microphone from the patrol car radio in his hand while he placed the suspect's left hand on the passenger side spot light and began asking a series of innocuous questions; name, age, race, marital status; all the while the light on the radio remained green.

Richard congratulated him on his truthfulness and then asked him if he'd duck napped Waldo from the backyard pen.

"No, I didn't duck nap no duck, I tole y'all he was just awalkin' down the sidewalk when I come to help him out."

Richard depressed the mike talk key and immediately the green light went out and, in its place, the red light began to glow.

"OOOO nooo, the machine senses an untruth in your answer, you must be guilty and we're going to have to take you to jail!"

The three-mile trip to the station began with Richard keying the mike again to advise his dispatcher that they had a prisoner in custody. At the same instant the duck began to quack uproariously, drowning out Richard. The astute radio operator didn't miss a beat as she asked; 'Supervisor unit with traffic, please repeat your message?"

The rest of the trip was spent in silence and after leaving the patrol car in the station parking lot; the two deputies walked the duck napper into the booking area and locked him in a stout open wire holding cell as they left momentarily to tell the on-duty sergeant about their arrest and to get his advice about holding a live duck as evidence.

As they walked away, the duck napper asked them a question that brought a smile to both of their faces.

"It was me that found Waldo the Talking Duck! Maybe you can get that reward money for me so's I can use it for my bail???"

SCUBA KING

by Duane T. Preimsberger, Assist. Sheriff, retired

Firestone Sheriff's Station was located at the corner of Nadeau St. and Compton Ave. in South Central Los Angeles. It was a busy place with plenty of interesting people and law enforcement issues with which to deal. In 1963 I was assigned there as a rookie trainee, my training officer, Almus Stewart, was a seasoned veteran of the streets. It was his job to try and mold me into a competent patrol deputy who could be turned loose and alone into the area.

Almus had his hands full making sure that I was capable of handling radio call, making arrests and writing reports as well as patrolling the area on the lookout for the unusual.

Sometimes the unusual came to us via the most routine of radio calls. One day watch mid-morning Almus and I were working Car 12 in the north end of our station area. The radio came alive with our call letters and directed us to handle a suspicious person's incident. As the dispatcher began to give us a physical description, I stopped writing and began to smile as I learned it wouldn't be too difficult to locate this guy!

"Male white, approximately 35- 40 years old, 5'10", 165 pounds, blonde hair, subject is wearing a white tee shirt, a newspaper delivery bag and blue jeans. Subject also has on a scuba mask and swim flippers. Last seen eastbound on 71 St. from Compton Ave. going door to door," said the dispatcher."

Almus looked at me with a little smirk on his face. "Buddy, he must be a relative of yours from the beach I suppose?" In those days I lived in Seal Beach, a small ocean front town about 25 miles from the station.

"Nope, if he was one of my relatives, he'd be carrying a boogie board, I'm not into scuba, besides the equipment is pretty expensive."

"Well, you still get to talk to him; I'm not very good at communicating in that ocean jive!"

We pulled to the curb on 71 St. just as our subject completed the delivery of a throwaway newspaper to the front door of one of the homes on the street. As he turned and began his walk down the pathway to the sidewalk it was all I could do to keep from laughing.

The subject stared at us from within a scuba mask and as he walked his swim fins slapped the sidewalk announcing each of his steps. Even Almus, who usually had great emotional control, began chuckling to himself. "O.K. beach boy, you handle this one.

I'm just going to stand by and watch."

"Good morning sir. We received a call about you from a concerned resident so I'll have to ask you what business you have here in the neighborhood."

The face behind the scuba mask brightened and soon I had my answer. "I'm a deliveryman for Daily Door to Door, I'm dropped off with these here newspapers; see I got a whole bunch left in my sack and there's others in piles on corners waiting for me. I even got a card with my name and picture on it that says I'm an employee. I ain't never had one a them before."

"What's your name sir?"

"Washington Monroe Jackson, my momma named me after presidents she knew I'd grow up to be famous, but you can call me Scuba King!"

"Alright Mr. King, can I ask why you're wearing a scuba mask and swim fins, and incidentally, I noticed your mask doesn't seem to have any glass in it?" "Tidal waves dude, you just never know when a giant Tsunami might wallop the coast and if and when it does, I'll be ready."

"What about the glass?" "Fog dude!" "Fog?"

"Ya, fog; when I walks a long way with the glass in the mask it gets all fogged up no matter how much spit I rub on the inside. So, I pop out the glass and keep it handy right here in my sack. Ya wanna see it?"

"Thanks, I don't think so." "How long have you had this job?"

"A long time, almost a month, I really like it 'cause I'm outside all day in the sunshine and if it rains, I can just put on my wet suit."

"Have the police ever stopped you before?"

"Seems like I talks to them every day and they asks me the same questions you'all do."

"They ever take you to jail?" "Nope, but one cop made me get in his car and then he dropped me off about five miles from my route that day. The dude almost got me fired."

I ran a want and warrant check on Mr. Washington Monroe Jackson, aka Scuba King, and found out that there was no reason to detain him. He looked unusual but wasn't violating any laws. After a brief conversation with Almus I told him I was going to let Scuba King go."

He smiled and replied, "Good choice beach boy."

We said good bye to this unusual guy and watched and smiled as he slapped and flapped on down the sidewalk toward his next delivery, then he stopped and turned toward us with some advice."

"Dudes, if the big wave hits, watch out for the kelp you can get tangled up in it and drown." "Thanks Scuba King, we'll try and remember that!"

WEST HOLLYWOOD STATION 1971-1972

Sgt. John Jackson, LASD, retired

Every story in WHD is different from the normal. As a young naive deputy to the Hollywood life style in the early in 1971-72, I was taken back often by strange and stranger incidents. My first week was a real learning experience with arrest off the boulevard of drunk and disturbing young people. One of those was a young lady well painted with makeup and swanky clothes, appearing to be a hooker. At the booking counter I called for the matron to search the young hooker type that I had in custody. The matron investigated and called me back to the booking cage and said, this is a male, so have at it, pointing out loudly so everyone could laugh at me. WOW! To think I would have probably moved on this one had I encountered her in a social setting.

As my experienced rose in the land of enchantment, I was informed that a local club called "the Farm" was operating a young run-away juvenile hang out and operating after hours. On one early morning around 3 a.m. I led a group of my friendly patrol partners to the location. Loud music was heard but the doors were closed and locked. The music stopped upon our loud knocking, but no response. Not being one to back down, I wedged the front push bar on the bumper of my radio car against the door and knocked it in, to which the Calvary made entry. We made numerous arrests for minors, mostly wanted runaways, and wrote citations to the establishment for a variety of violations. As I was walking around the dance floor checking ID's, a young man tapped me on the shoulder and said "might we dance." With that invitation, I danced him out the door by the knap of the collar and seat of the pants to a waiting patrol car for transportation to the infamous portals of the booking gage at the station.

Following the above episode, the gays marched on the station the next day in protest of my actions and those of my partners. When I came to work that evening to work the EM shift, I was immediately summoned to the Captain's office (Capt. Arial for an ass chewing and don't do this again. The stigma eventually resided, and I later became a Special Crime Activity Team (SCAT) leader, five members and a Sergeant Tatsch Another great experience of working a variety of enforcement scenarios, which was the beginning of "Community Policing" in the West Hollywood area. There is a blue manual someplace that talks about this program.

415B CHASEN'S RESTAURANT
by Gary Fitzgerald

We received a 415B call at the restaurant with the usual HBD customer irate about parking. We made nice nice and told the fella to hit the bricks. An older gentleman wearing a suit came over and asked us if we would like dinner. We had heard that Howard Hughes like the chili there so we stopped to have dinner. The maître d' seated us in the middle of the house. The wine captain was next and finally the waiter. The folks at the table across from us were quite upset that we were dining in uniform next to them. The maître d' was summoned and he returned with the man in the suit. It turns out that he was the owner, Dave Chasen. The only thing he said was, "there is my place, please leave the restaurant."

I guess the patron didn't like law enforcement. They picked up their stuff and left in a huff. The parking lot incident had nothing to do with dinner. That was the best chili I ever had.

ELVIS & I

by Steve Lee

My all-time favorite, though, was a call at the Rainbow Room where my partner and I were able to log an assist by Elvis Presley... the real King, not an impersonator.

We had responded to a 415-drunk call at "the Rainbow Room" over the Roxy Theater at about 2100 hours and found that due to lack of parking (remember the lack of parking?) we left our black and white on the median of the Sunset Strip with the rotators going. We elbowed our way through the overflow crowd waiting to get into the Roxy and Rainbow Room and found the obnoxious subject of our call leaning against a nearby wall mother f***in everything under the sun. While we were dealing with this guy, a hush fell over the crowd. I turned and saw a dark-haired man in a stark white karate outfit approaching as the crowd parted around him like the waters of the Red Sea. He had half a dozen of his" helpers" in tow behind him and a .45 automatic tucked into his belt. The belt, it's worth noting, was not just a black belt like you might see on a karate master but was multicolored with various stripes. Turns out that Elvis had been coming down Sunset Blvd in his limousine convoy and had seen our patrol car parked on the median. He had decided to take action. "You boys need some help?" said Elvis in his instantly recognizable voice, and then, "here, let me take care of this for you." He strode up to our drunk and to our utter amazement the mouth on the source of our call suddenly went silent. Even in his inebriated state he recognized who was addressing him. Elvis proceeded to read this guy the riot act, waving his finger in the miscreant's wide-eyed face. Once he had sufficiently cowed the individual, he turned back to us. At that particular time, I was very interested in martial arts and had studied Tang Soo Do Karate at the Chuck Norris studio in Lakewood. Elvis and I proceeded to talk about the various styles of karate (turns out he had fashioned his own bizarre looking karate belt) and it was during this exchange that my law enforcement training slipped back into gear. I couldn't help noticing that despite the dimly lit environment, Elvis's pupils were screwed down tight. My first inclination was that the King was on drugs .... but then I thought... nawwww... how could that be? This is the anti-drug "special agent" photographed with Nixon in the Oval Office .... but what else could explain his objective symptoms? I took a second look at the gun in his waistband and just for a moment a scenario played out in my mind where I would hook him up and frog march him out to our unit . . . . but then thought better of it due to the publicity shit storm that would inevitably follow. By this time word of mouth had brought a huge flood of onlookers and traffic was backing up on Sunset. One of Elvis's entourage tapped him on the shoulder. The King offered his hand to me, I shook it and then off he went, parting the crowd once again. It wasn't until this moment that I noticed he had "Elvis" emblazoned on the back of his outfit. Not a shrinking violet, this guy. I've always regretted that I didn't make a Xerox a copy of my log for that night but looking back I have to remember that the spectacular and the unusual were pretty much everyday occurrences when I worked West Hollywood.

Steve Lee

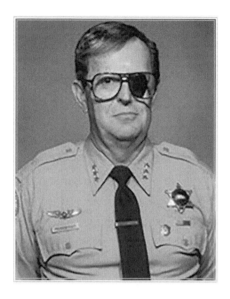

SMELLS LIKE A DEAD GUY

By Duane Preimsberger, Assist. Sheriff, retired

I got up at 6 am and tried not to wake up my wife and two little girls as I prepared to work the day watch from 8 am – p.m. at Firestone Sheriffs
station in south central Los Angeles. The drive from Seal Beach wasn't too bad and I was at the station and dressed in my uniform well before the start on my shift.

I was assigned to car 17, a one-man unit assigned to the south end of our stations area. Usually, the days began with a flurry of reports from the victims of thefts and a number of calls to persons injured or sick who needed medical attention. I loaded up my patrol car with my patrol box that contained

all the blank report forms I might need as well as addition ammo for my service revolver and the shotgun that was held in a rack along the floor in front of the front seat, additionally I had some personal items like breath mints, a tape measure, heavy duty gloves and a jar of Vicks.

The first few minutes of the shift were quiet with little two-way radio traffic for me or units adjoining my area. Then the usual happened and the work for the day began. The dispatcher gave me three calls and advised me to handle them in the order they were dispatched. First was a possible 927d (a dead body), next up was a residential burglary report and last was a petty theft report. I headed for the dead body call expecting that a family member had gone to bed feeling fine and had passed away in their sleep. That was not to be the case. Instead, I found myself in a rundown trailer park where a sleepy-eyed manager stood outside the office trailer awaiting my arrival. She filled me in and told me that the trailer in space number 10 was unlocked with the door wide open and no one answering her knock. In addition, the smell emanating from the inside of the trailer was nauseating and she was pretty certain that the single guy who lived there had died. I thanked her and explained that I'd check things out and let her know what was to be done.

Space number 10 was filled with a small aluminum travel type trailer. Perhaps 15 feet long and maybe 8 feet wide, it had a single door and as the manager had advised it was fully open. After parking my patrol car, I got out and began to approach the open door and as I got close, I smelled something bad and I hoped it wasn't a decomposing human being. It was pretty powerful and I decided to employ a technique I'd learned from an experienced homicide detective. I got the jar of Vicks out of my patrol box and applied a goodly portion to the inside of both of my nostrils and –presto- the smell was covered by the aroma of Vicks. I knocked and yelled but got no response so I let myself into the front room, that served as part living room, dining area and kitchen.

A narrow hallway led to a bathroom area and tiny bedroom and it was in the bedroom that I found a body and the source of the pungent odor. A white male, probably in his late 30's, lay fully clothed on his back on the bed. He had on a blue sweat shirt, blue jeans, work boots and a rubberized apron that reached to his knees. I began inspecting the body to confirm that it was in fact dead. The first thing I wanted to do was to check the guys eyes with my flashlight to assure that there wouldn't be any pupillary response to the light beam. Since his eyes were closed, I opened one of them and immediately got the hell scared out of me. The guy on the bed wasn't dead and instead he was quite alive and grumpy that some stranger was fooling around with his face. His scream, coupled with his grabbing my hand caused me to vault backward and in doing so I destroyed the thin sliding particle board door that served to conceal a small closet. It took a minute before the two of us were able to gain control of our emotions. Since I was standing up, I got to tell my story first and I explained how I had arrived at his home. I was amazed when he started to smile at my tale and then he began to laugh. It was then that I realized that my activity there wasn't going to end with a citizen's complaint against me and I breathed a sigh of relief. Then it was time to hear the I ain't dead guys story.

Larry Anderson lived in the trailer and had been there for a couple of years. He worked in San Pedro at a fish cannery and over the last two days had been dealing with a crisis at work. Some miserable, low-life, creep had dumped a couple of tons of rotting fish in front of their loading dock, and this stunt had almost closed down their operations. Larry was one of the guys who shared the responsibility of cleaning up the mess by loading the rotten fish in a big dumpster, hauling it away to an incinerator, burning it into ashes and then taking the ashes to the dump. He smelled especially bad because of his close contact with the rotten fish. He apologized for upsetting his landlady and having the cops come out. He was exhausted after having worked two consecutive 16-hour days at hard labor and that's why he had crashed on his bed. I too smiled and laughed at Larry's tale and I was especially glad that he was OK and that I wouldn't be writing a person dead report. I was on my way out of the trailer when Larry stopped me as he opened up the freezer compartment of his small refrigerator and provided me with two big lobster tails to make up for having to stick Vicks up my nose!

ABOUT THE AUTHOR

Love-Et' KayPulls is my pen name. I am 77 years old. Law Enforcement was my life. I have always been a very silly person and find it difficult to be serious even at times when it is not appropriate. That is the main reason I never chose to go into the clergy. Unfortunately, I would have opened every sermon with a dirty joke. I seem unable to control the things that come out of my mouth.

Sometime in 2019 I am planning to host a 50-year reunion in Las Vegas for my Sheriff's academy classmates. It should be fun to see who is still around. After all, none of us are "Spring Chickens" anymore. We will all have to wear name tags because after 50 years, we wouldn't recognize each other if we bumped into each other on the street.

I'm considering hiring a 25-year-old "Hottie" to pretend to be me, just to blow everyone's mind. When anyone tells her that she looks too young to be me, I'll have her tell them that I just had a facelift.

19-years ago, I met a very nice young man, 28-years my junior. We are still together. But that is another book in itself.

I HOPE YOU ENJOYED YOUR TRIP WITH ME.